Freedom and Fairness

Trade unions in Britain have undergone a double ordeal since 1979. Mass unemployment has diminished their bargaining power in many sectors, often weakening their actual membership, and eroding their funds. At the same time, there has been an unprecedented legal assault calculated to impose many restrictions on union behaviour. These two pressures have forced unions to think and respond politically.

Naturally they hope that a new Labour Government will provide a more favourable economic and social climate. Specifically, they expect that the rights and immunities which have been taken away will be restored in a more reliable form, so they can begin to represent their members effectively again. This has been a matter of intense debate in the TUC and Labour Party. The discussions leading up to the latest documents are carefully charted and considered in *Freedom and Fairness, Empowering People at Work*.

Without an adequate legal framework, unions will not be able to operate freely. But to regain the social initiative they must do far more than simply regain their former legal status. To recover power, unions need to create a new internationalism, capable of responding to transnational economic power. They need to reach into constituencies from which they have hitherto been excluded. They need to acquire a capacity to initiate actions, and shape a future, rather than simply responding to attacks, and defending the past. This book begins to explore these wider problems and perspectives.

FREEDOM

and

FAIRNESS

Empowering People at Work

edited by Ken Coates

with contributions from Stephen Bodington,
Ken Coates, John Edmonds, Bob Fryer, Roy Green,
Stuart Holland MP, John Hughes,
Emma MacLennan, Jim Mortimer, Andrew Wilson

foreword by John Prescott MP

Spokesman
for the
Institute for Workers' Control

First published in 1986 by:
Spokesman
Bertrand Russell House
Gamble Street
Nottingham, England
Tel. 0602 708318

Humanities Press International inc.
Atlantic Highlands, New Jersey 07716, USA

ISBN 0-85124-440-8 Hardcase
ISBN 0-85124-450-5 Paperback

Printed by the Russell Press Ltd (TU), Nottingham

Contents

Contents

Foreword

John Prescott MP, Shadow Employment Spokesperson

The debate on the future of labour law and industrial relations in Britain has entered new and uncharted waters.

The Tories have torn up the rules governing the post-war settlement between capital and labour. They have made anti-union legislation a centrepiece of their whole economic stretegy, deliberately shutting workers out of key decisions and taking away basic rights to fair treatment.

The consequences for our people have been disastrous, but there is no going back to a mythical golden age of 'voluntarism'. I do not believe that it is possible or even desirable to attempt to exclude the law from industrial relations.

The recent experiences of trade unions such as the TGWU and the AEU have shown that the courts have become much more determined to impose sanctions for non-compliance with greater use of sequestrators and receivers. The Government's anti-trade union legislation and the movement response has allowed it to be presented as if we are against individual rights and indifferent to membership participation in ballots.

What we as a movement must do is decide how best to frame *new* legislation so that it gives maximum support to both individual workers and their unions. Labour now has the chance for the first time in a generation to rewrite the political agenda. We must seize it.

A start has been made with the statements agreed this year between the Labour Party and the TUC on industrial relations and low pay. They go some way to spelling out the themes of freedom and fairness at work which up to now have been vague to say the least. Of course, further discussion will be needed to develop a more detailed programme, especially in our proposed fair wages strategy and the extension of industrial democracy as a basis of economic policy and planning.

That is why I welcome the publication of this book, which contributes to the wider discussion of these issues within the movement. No discussion can ever be final or complete; ours will continue well beyond the next election and the one after that.

It remains a hard truth, however, that if our ideas and proposals are to have any practical meaning, we must use them to win power. We can then look forward to an extended period of social reform, in which working people themselves are able to plan for jobs, growth and social justice.

I
Introduction

Trade unions in Britain have undergone a double ordeal since 1979. Mass unemployment has diminished their bargaining power in many sectors, often weakening their actual membership, and eroding their funds. At the same time, there has been an unprecedented legal assault calculated to impose many restrictions on union behaviour. These two pressures have forced unions to think and respond politically. In turn, the politics can operate at two levels: the level of the demand for new legal institutions, and the level of political campaigning to win over public support for trade union objectives.

Traumatic arguments have taken place in Britain, but these are part of a European upheaval. Transnational economic power has gathered strength and influence over all the continent, undermining the capacity of national governments to control their economic affairs. Trade Unions need to co-ordinate their efforts internationally to create an answering strategy.

Chapter 1

Freedom and Fairness in Peril

Ken Coates

Throughout Western Europe unemployment has been rising. Slower growth rates have met the population 'bulge', and in 1985 some nineteen million people were officially registered as unemployed. The true number of workless people is, of course, substantially higher. Procedures for registration vary from one country to another. Often young people are not registered in any adequate way. Women may be excluded from the count when there is discrimination in their registration procedures. Even on the official counts, however, 11 per cent of employable Europeans are now without jobs. In some countries the proportions are not so bad: but this only means other countries suffer more drastically. Sweden confines its unemployment to less than 3 per cent of the active population, and Austria can keep it down to 5 per cent. But in Spain, 22.3 per cent are workless, in the Netherlands the figure runs at 14.4 per cent, and in Belgium at 13.1 per cent. This may be compared with the British total of 11.8 per cent. Of course, just as the rates fluctuate across the continent, so they also vary internally. Certain regions, and certain industries are hit particularly hard.

All this has dealt ferocious blows against trade unionism, even if different unions have been differentially affected. In Britain not only is there a disproportionately high level of unemployment in certain regions, but the collapse of sectors of manufacturing industry has resulted in severe membership loss in certain major unions. In the first half of the 1980s, union membership overall in Britain fell by 14.4 per cent, or almost double the rate of fall in levels of employment. Serious membership losses have afflicted particular unions, notably the Transport and General Workers' Union. Others have been undermined, including some in what were formerly some of the most highly organized sectors. Weaker unions have been going to the wall. In the production and construction industries, union membership fell by almost one-third in the first four years of the decade. There had been seven million workers in British manufacturing industry in 1979, but this number declined to 5.4 million by mid-1985. The growth in employment in service sectors was insufficient to absorb those displaced, leave alone the wave of school-leavers.

In 1985, wages rose faster than prices, and real earnings rose faster than wage rates. This fact persuades many people that collective bargaining is still alive and well. Perhaps such judgements should be treated with a little caution. How far have wage rises been traded against flexibility in working arrangements? What have they represented in terms of technological adaptation, demarcation, adjustments of manning levels? How far have changes in pay levels been linked to assessments of 'merit'? The evaluation of the precise weight of trade union influence is not a simple matter.

What is clear is that trade unions have been sensing the need for a turn towards more political forms of action. The level of strike activity has been falling, and in the private sector it has reached bottom. All the biggest strikes and disputes have raged in the public sector, affecting not only miners, but teachers and other local authority employees. This concentration, which flows from governmental discrimination against public employees, is itself a political event. In very different environments, there has been intensified industrial conflict with public sector workers in other countries, from Austria up to the Netherlands, or Sweden. Incomes policies, wage freezes, tax reforms, and changes in the social wage have all become issues in one country after another, and this development has also intensified the shift to a political focus.

In Britain this shift has been filtered through a mesh imposed by the 1984 Trade Union Act. This mesh was carefully calculated to exploit divisions within the unions, seeking to mobilize 'the silent majority' of trade union members against activist local leaders, and to foment conflicts between activists and national leaders. Resolutely set against 'interventionism' in industrial affairs, Mrs Thatcher's team has watched the disappearance of whole sectors of the British economy without moving a muscle. But there has been no such thing as non-intervention in the field of trade union competence.

The 1984 Act imposed regulations over three distinct areas of trade union government. First, it regulated elections to trade union executive committees. Second, it provided for the institution of strike ballots, subject to a penalty involving the removal of immunities if strikes were called without ballots.

Thirdly, it sought to regulate trade union political funds, by imposing a decennial ballot as a condition for the renewal of such funds.

Strong efforts were made by the Government to influence the resultant political fund ballots, but without success. Every union which had already established a political fund voted, in the event, to continue it. Indeed, subsequently, four unions which previously lacked any such fund, have now decided to establish one. The percentage of trade unionists voting to continue their funds was in no case less than 70, and commonly ran in the middle or high 80s. These results had been won by a very systematic campaign, in which trade union leaders at the national level organized extensive consultations and briefings with their activists, and set about an intense joint labour of persuasion of the rank and file membership. In this one case, the attack of Mrs Thatcher's Government actually compelled the unions to close their ranks, and in doing so they won their first major victory in what had been a season of demoralizing defeats.

The 1984 Act was to prove more damaging in its other provisions. Ostensibly aimed at greater democracy, these provisions were really intended to disaggregate collective strength. We have discussed this strategy in detail elsewhere*. In order to extend democracy in trade unions, there are two roads to reform. It can be done voluntarily, from below, as a result of deliberate choices and persuasion. Or it can be attempted by governmental regulation. However, for this second option to succeed, it would be necessary to extend democracy in industry as a whole. If workers enjoyed truly human rights in their work, they would need to arrange their unions in such a way as to take up such rights. But where industry is still an unaccountable autocracy, rights are still indecisively established, if they are not actually denied. In a word, you get the rights you can fight for. The very language of battle and conflict calls up images of authority and military organization. Of course, unions are not armies, and in the last analysis they must always unite their members by a process of persuasion, but if their constitutional powers are arbitrarily restricted by the need to operate in a fundamentally undemocratic territory, then their capacity for persuasion will be adversely affected in the process.

The 1984 Act was by no means the only harmful intervention of the Thatcher Government in the domain of industrial relations. Necessarily, the political perspective of the Trade Union Congress became hooked on the need to lift the wide variety of

---

*Ken Coates, Tony Topham: *Trade Unions and Politics*, Basil Blackwell, 1986.

curbs imposed upon its members since 1979. The issue of repeal is really deeply important. But it would be a savage paradox if it blanked out discussion on the other wide-ranging reforms which are needed by the labour movement. Mrs Thatcher's revenge for her defeat would then come from watching our obsession with the clearing away of her debris, while we neglected the construction of our own frameworks. Without such new frameworks, carefully designed to contend with the changed balance of power which results from mass unemployment, the trade unions will remain far weaker than they ought to be, if a robust democracy is to survive in Britain, at a time of disastrous economic performance, and continuing crisis.

Not surprisingly negotiations between the TUC and the Labour Party have gone ahead with some difficulty. The straightforward repeal of the 1984 Act, some Labour leaders felt, might enable the Government to misrepresent the Labour Party as being indifferent to the rights of individual trade union members. Of course, the fundamental right of working people is the right to a job, and in the absence of that right all other rights shrink, if they do not actually disappear altogether. It would be possible through legislation to buttress workpeople's collective powers, and a large part of this book is concerned with the question of how to do this. But this question cannot be posed against the need to repeal those measures which have been inimical to the work of the unions. Foremost amongst these measures has been the 1984 Act, which receives very much more detailed attention below. Here, we are concerned only with the general principles of its operation against the labour movement.

Trade union democracy has never been reducible to balloting, important though electoral processes are within it. The representation of workpeople is a quite different and more dynamic process from that involved in geographical constituencies. At the workplace, when one elects a shop steward, the democratic initiative has only just begun, while in Parliamentary and municipal elections the vote is all too often the last active involvement in which the electorate has any influence whatever. The new shop steward finds his constituency is continuously present, making tangible responses to events as they happen. The dialogue between leaders and led is mutually influential, because it is above all direct.

Things are not so straightforward higher up the union hierarchies. True, access to representatives may remain close and easy, and individual and group influences on collective decisions may be more marked than it is in the political process. But because unions are national entities, they also need formal channels of communication and accountability, and this implies regular election of leading bodies. It does not, however, necessarily imply the strict imposition of a standard mode of representation: different industries have different structures, and the elaboration of their democratic procedures needs room to reflect and represent these structures. There are a variety of legitimate models of trade union democracy, and not the least of the faults of the 1984 Trade Union Act was that it was simplistic in its approach to these.

Unions were not constituted as electoral machines, but as representative mechanisms. As more and more of the vital work of industrial representation has devolved on the workplace, so national organization has sometimes become more difficult. In some unions, the structure of branches has, in practice, become attenuated, because effective decisions on the most urgent matters have been the prerogative of shop stewards. This would not have mattered if the same shop stewards had also received the custody of constitutional representation, or if the responsibilities had, in some way, also passed over from geographical branches to enterprise-based units. To conduct an effective postal ballot of a million members, for instance, one needs a million correct names and addresses. Upon whom falls the duty of maintaining this? In general elections, we use the results of the work of professional registration officers, and even though these maintain an expensive service, it is sometimes found to be gravely faulty. In unions, which often collect subscriptions through check-off systems administered by employers, even the addresses of members may be difficult to determine. If the task of compiling lists is to fall on voluntary branch officers, it is likely to make it difficult to recruit such volunteers, and nearly certain that the resultant roles will be inadequately maintained. This will be all the more true when involvement in branch life is restricted to a handful of members while the real work of representation is done outside the branch. We should remember that no less a person than George Woodcock used to say that if he were starting life in the union during the '60s, he would not be interested in branch meetings, but would instead seek to become a shop steward. Yet the constitutional role of the branches (in which "you would not catch me", as Woodcock said) remained quite crucial in determining national election procedures. The 1984 Act did nothing to resolve such problems. It would have been much easier for would-be reformers to go with the grain of workshop organization, and to legislate to compel employers to provide adequate facilities for workplace electioneering and balloting.

This would extend personal rights at the same time that it facilitated collective organization. But this would have involved a growth in democracy, rather than a subversion of 'democratic' rhetoric to the purposes of disrupting union solidarity.

But the issue of trade union elections is quite distinct from that of ballots on particular actions, such as that of strike ballots. The question here is different. A worker who enrols in a union has decided to join his personal fortunes with others in order to secure a collective settlement to his claims, which he anticipates, will bring him an advantage over any likely personal settlement. His rights in such a case depend upon effective representation, competent negotiation, and a responsive leadership. Collective bargaining may result in failure to agree, and that may result in various kinds of sanctions, not excluding strikes. But although the sanctions are present (as a possibility) in the field of force within which negotiation takes place, they are not an inevitable outcome, even if talks fail. At the same time, their possibility is part of the inducement brought to bear on employers to settle. Sanctions are normally easier to apply in times of full employment: but then they are less necessary, because competition for scarce labour is itself an inducement to meet union claims. With mass unemployment, sanctions become more difficult to apply. Workers are likely to become more defensive, more cautious, and less 'militant' when they are surrounded by millions in dole queues. This change happens, not because they have been given the 'right' to moderate their opinions and behaviour, but because they have been *denied* the right to full employment and protection against unfair competition in the job market. To compel strike ballots in such circumstances is to further weaken bargaining power without conferring any positive rights whatever. The result gives employers the right to call a union's bluff, and to defer any settlement until they have determined whether they might encounter serious opposition or not. A union's bluff might not often be worth much, with four million out-of-work people all around: but to agree an employer's right to call it is not a rational way to address such an imbalance. Even to leave the initiative to union members may be to undermine vestigial bargaining rights, if employers can encourage or provoke membership litigation.

Of course, unions often need strike ballots. They are a way of testing the water: sometimes they are even a way of educating opinion. But the danger of people being "forced to strike against their will" is largely chimerical: strikes are declining in numbers, extension, and effect, not because of the 1984 Act, but because of the economic blizzard which rages over the industrial landscape.

The far more pressing danger is still further erosion of bargaining power and initiative, which will directly wear down the right to negotiate reasonable conditions of work and acceptable rewards. When a union needs strike ballots, it should certainly conduct them. If it is foolish enough to call strikes when people do not want to respond, it will pay a bitter price for its folly. But a compulsion to ballot, in this case, is a compulsion to show all its cards to the adversary, before bargaining is half-way to concluded. If the next Labour Government could deal better cards to all our workpeople in the shape of the restoration of full employment, quickly, such ballots would have no ill-effect. But if full employment is a long way off, then strike ballots should once again be made voluntary options, usable at the entire discretion of unions and their members.

A new strike wave is distinctly unlikely unless the trade union movement is reduced to actual desperation. Widespread strikes do not correlate easily with mass unemployment. The real question for the unions is how to recover, on the political plane, influence and power which they have lost in the industrial field. That is the main concern of this collection of papers, which have been prepared in a series of seminars organized by the Institute for Workers' Control. But these papers, although they address a range of possible measures designed to meet this need, do not in so doing seek to re-enter a world that has gone beyond recall. We could not step back into 1979 even if we wished to.

The Institute is in as strong a position as anyone to understand the extent to which trade unions have been weakened during the Thatcher years. At the same time, the need for a self-managing society is actually increased by economic crisis. While the workers' movement is undoubtedly weakened by mass unemployment, the need for change is intensified. These processes compel us to widen the range of our arguments, and to seek more cosmopolitan linkages. We have already argued the need for joint local action, on an international scale, as part of the struggle for economic recovery. In the same way, the struggle for greater industrial democracy also acquires its international dimensions.

Can we say that the crisis has brought us into a more political world? Certainly trade unionists will not find remedies for the injustices they suffer, unless they can unite their forces in political actions conceived on a broad scale. Community action, too, becomes ever more difficult as funding for local initiatives is withdrawn: so that the recasting of social priorities, a profoundly political process, becomes a pre-condition for success. The growth of transnational economic power undermines the democratic initiatives of Governments themselves. Democrats who yesterday combined their forces in local associations and workplace trade unions, now find that action on the national political level is insufficient, and that for many purposes, international co-operation becomes essential.

The British labour movement is only beginning to explore the new agenda which all this implies. Of course, we cannot walk away from the responsibility of facing the immediate practical issues, such as those addressed in this book. But as the patterns of economic power evolve, so must the scale of our responses.

Partly this is a matter of co-operation within existing frameworks. But partly it requires that we create new institutions, and new campaigns, in which a new internationalism becomes manifest. The trade unions will not recover on a purely national plane, even if a new Labour Government introduces optimal legislation on industrial democracy. The enlargement of trade union rights of representation and joint determination, or the imposition of mandatory planning agreements, or any of the other devices which are explored below, will all take place within structures which are part of transnational enterprise. How will unions operate their new powers, if they do not have their international trade union partnerships to reinforce them? If half a dozen European Governments institute planning agreements under half a dozen different names, at what point do both Governments and unions bring their separate acts together, to confront what will, all the time, remain the single company which is the object of all their separate attentions? If Europe, or the world, had a Government, then legislation for planning agreements would enable a centralized democracy, operating according to all the standard liberal prescriptions, to treat with that commercial power and render it accountable. But where a plurality of democratic authorities enter separate relations with one authoritarian power, they may easily expect to be worsted.

Mass unemployment can be reduced, but full employment will not be restored until we can pose against transnational economic power an integrated international democratic force. Innumerable constituencies begin to share in international perspectives. The women's movement; the peace movements; ecologists and environmentalists: all are corresponding one with another, and meeting in a variety of impromptu fora up and down the European continent. The socialist parties have been working to create a programme of convergent action, which has been carefully argued in *Global Challenge*, the Manley-Brandt Report.

The European Trade Union Confederation is rapidly becoming

the most effective and integrated of all the trade union internationals, and it is providing an invaluable focus on real issues, such as that of working time.

If all these forces could come together, we should begin a new epoch. Until they do, the most powerful institutions will remain above the reach of national law, and will arrange, among themselves, what is to be, and what is not to be, in the international order. But British workers did not create the incredible variety in their union organisations in order to be so easily contained. Together with their colleagues in all the other countries, they will surely reach forward to create the basis for an alternative Europe, and an alternative world.

II
Legislation
for
Freedom and Fairness

The Conservative Governments since 1979 have shown great skill in framing industrial relations legislation, and have learnt many lessons from the disastrous mistakes of the 1970 Heath administration. Of course, the new laws of the 1980s took effect at a time of mass (and rising) unemployment. Such a time was bound to be difficult, even demoralising for the unions. By cleverly intervening to remove legal protection from whole categories of union action, the Government shifted the balance of power in industry very decisively towards the employers. The removal of union 'immunities' left the Government free to claim that its policy was 'non-interventionist'. But such 'non-interventionism' was to be joined by heavy interference in the processes of union government, with legislation to 'democratise' union organisation. The 1984 Trade Union Act was designed to exploit divisions between leaders, activists and ordinary members, and using 'democratic' slogans in a work of disaggregation.

The Institute for Workers' Control in considering how to respond to all this legislation, convened a series of meetings in which the following papers were presented. They seek to explore the methods by which freedom of trade union action may be restored, at the same time as new industrial powers begin to enable working people to exert a real influence over the content of their lives at work.

Chapter 2

The Debate over Labour Law: New Rights or New Responsibilities?

Andrew Wilson

The Crisis in the Labour Movement

Following the Second Congress in 1903 of the Russian Social-Democratic Labour Party, which established the supremacy of the Bolshevik faction and its principles of organisation, the "opportunist" elements in the Party re-grouped, gained control of its newspaper, *Iskra*, and used it to attack the Central Committee. Lenin described the course of events as "one step forward, two steps back", a demonstration of the fact that "development does indeed proceed dialectically, by way of contradictions"[1]. The labour movement in Britain, however, is different. It is not an organisation of professional revolutionaries independent of the working people whose interests it represents. It does not make daring intellectual advances in strategy and principle before relapsing into established practices and habits which precipitate a crisis. On the contrary, it first allows itself to be overtaken by crisis and then instinctively takes two steps backwards. Only then does it become possible to take a step forward. The ground shifts and the old edifice collapses — necessity is then the mother of invention.

These days, of course, nearly everybody is in favour of some sort of change and therefore claims to be 'progressive' in relation to what already exists. Who will admit to stepping backwards? The 'Thatcher Revolution', despite its espousal of the 'return to Victorian values', did not openly advocate a return to the conditions of Victorian society. Rather, the implicit claim was that the economic progress of the 20th century would permit those values to be enjoyed by a greater number of people, including the skilled working class, if only the out-dated constraints which had developed in reaction to the poverty and insecurity of the 19th century could be discarded. Having outlived their usefulness, they operated as a brake upon further progress which, as always, rested upon the enhancement of individual freedom. What was promised was a great leap forward.

Similarly, the 'Kinnock Revolution' in the Labour Party following the election defeat in June 1983, although openly espousing 'moderation' and a shift towards the political centre, has also been carried through under the banner of 'modernisation'. Social progress, in part the result of Labour's own policies, has undermined its traditional base of support and led to the emergence of the 'modern working classes' whose chief characteristic is their 'upward social mobility'. This does not exclude "active sympathy with the plight of the disadvantaged", but it does require, on the part of the labour movement, a "shift in attitudes and presentation". Central to the new vision of 'democratic socialism' is the value of 'individual freedom' — equality and democracy are now "the means which democratic socialism has chosen to protect that freedom"[2]. These are the themes of the Party's current "Freedom and Fairness" campaign. The task of the state is not to control and regulate, to direct the courses of social life; it is to ensure fair treatment, that the strong are not permitted to use their power oppressively, and, through the provision of basic collective services, that all are enabled to exercise real freedom.

To attack a perspective which seeks consciously to adapt Labour's position to the 'Thatcher revolution', and to stake out new ground therein simply as a 'retreat from socialism', assumes what is in dispute — the existence of a ready-made and eternally valid socialist conception. Judged by such a standard, it is inevitable that practical policies will fall short of the ideal. But does the ideal rest on anything more solid than faith and conviction? If we cast aside for present purposes the vagaries of political ideology as a yardstick, a more concrete standpoint from which to evaluate the current political trend of the Labour Party can be found in the trade union movement. The central thrust of the 'Thatcher revolution' has been its two-pronged attack on the unions. The destruction of the post-war consensus over full employment has seriously weakened them by direct loss of membership and bargaining power and also by accelerating long-run structural transformations in the workforce[3]. But the social and economic costs of this have been high. In contrast, the legal controls and restrictions imposed by the Employment Acts of 1980/82 and the 1984 Trade Union Act have been widely acclaimed as successful curbs upon excessive trade union power. The debate over labour law and the significance of the recently published TUC-Labour Party Liaison Committee documents[4] must be assessed within this context.

Origins of the Present Debate

Labour's policy on industrial relations legislation for the 1983 election was written entirely by the TUC. A document on *Repeal and Replacement Legislation* was approved by the General Council in February 1983 and rubber-stamped at the next meeting of the Liaison Committee in March. It called for the complete repeal of the Employment Acts and the restoration of the 'immunities' against common law liability for industrial action which had existed under the legislation of the previous Labour Government. Similarly, a section on union membership agreements provided explicitly that the law should be restored to its 1979 position, subject only to an exception to take account of the decision of the European Court of Human Rights in the *Young, James and Webster* case (1981). This had upheld the complaint brought by the former employees of British Rail that they should not have been compelled to join the National Union of Railwaymen (NUR) since they were not members of the union when the closed shop agreement was introduced.

Significantly, *Repeal and Replacement Legislation* was not intended to be published as a major political statement — there was no attempt to link it to broader themes. Even the industrial democracy policy developed in the 1982 statement on *Economic Planning and Industrial Democracy*[5] was mentioned only obliquely in a belated sentence suggesting that "the definition of 'trade dispute' on which the lawfulness of industrial action depends...should also include disputes about company policy which are not connected with terms and conditions of employment." The relatively low profile accorded to the repeal of the Tory labour law was in sharp contrast to the position in 1973-4 when the repeal of the discredited Industrial Relations Act formed a central plank of the 'Social Contract', which in turn formed a corner-stone of Labour's electoral and political strategy. A policy with a low profile is a weak policy. The reasons for this weakness can be found in the underlying strategy which sustained it.

The strength of the commitment to repeal the Industrial Relations Act rested on its failure to take root in the industrial relations system. The TUC's campaign of opposition was successful. On the eve of the election in February 1974, even

Campbell Adamson, Director-General of the Confederation of British Industry (CBI), called for the repeal of the Act, stating that it had "sullied" industrial relations. The way was clear for the Labour Party to carry into effect the strategy mapped out earlier in the majority report of the Donovan Royal Commission (1968), which itself reflected a much broader spectrum of views than the trade union movement alone. In fact, contrary to popular myth, the TUC was only with great difficulty persuaded to adopt this programme of reform. It seriously compromised and undermined, while professing to be consistent with, the tenet of 'voluntarism' or 'non-intervention' of the law in industrial relations, and it was conceived by many of its promoters as an adjunct to incomes policy. It is a distortion promoted energetically during this period by the press to say that the TUC "dictated" policy to the Labour Government, as though the latter was not also pursuing its own political interests.

The strategy supporting the policy of complete repeal of the Employment Acts was one of total opposition and non-compliance with the legislation, deriving its authority from the experience of the Industrial Relations Act. "The fact that trade unions generally adopted an aggressive posture", argued the paper submitted for approval to the conference of union executives at Wembley in April 1982, "made the Act unworkable." The Government, the TUC declared, "has forgotten or chosen to ignore the basic lessons of 1971." However, the tactical pivot on which the campaign against the 1971 Act rested was non-registration. The effect was to deny the unions any of the benefits conferred upon registered unions under the legislation and also to enlarge the scope of its punitive provisions. Thus the Act was not permitted to function as its framers had intended. By refusing to enter the legal universe which it attempted to create, the unions deliberately turned it into a case of drastic 'overkill'.

Two of the recommendations approved at Wembley sought to replicate the 1971 strategy. Affiliates were instructed not to participate in secret ballots on union membership agreements. The effect of this instruction not only confirmed the existing position that any closed shop agreements negotiated after the coming into force of the 1980 Act could not justify in law the dismissal of a worker on the grounds of non-membership of the relevant union. More importantly, it meant that no closed shop agreement would be able to operate within the law under the provisions of the 1982 Act requiring approval by at least an 85 per cent majority[6]. Secondly, unions were prohibited from applying for reimbursement for expenditure on ballots under the 1980 Act.

Again, this confirmation of the initial response to the Government's industrial relations strategy was designed to prevent unions gaining any benefits from the legislation, ensuring that they were all placed in the same unfavourable position to guarantee the unity of the movement. Raising the stakes in this way was a dangerous gamble. Unless there was a prospect that the legislation would soon be repealed, by increasing the damage which it inflicted and denying unions the benefits it offered, the strategy would be undermined by the development of pressure within the trade union movement to break ranks.

Even while it formally endorsed a repeat of the 1971 strategy, the Wembley document did not fail to recognise that in several crucial respects the legislation was different from its predecessor. It noted the absence of "any key provision on which the operation of the legislation as a whole will depend." No new court or other institution was created and nothing was dependent upon "unions themselves initiating actions or procedures." Instead, unions would simply be "on the receiving end of legal actions launched by others." The TUC document also noted, at a deeper level, the hostility of the economic and social context: rising levels of unemployment, especially in the traditional manufacturing areas, the cutting of public services, and the exclusion of unions from "any effective voice in the decisions which deeply affect working people." The hostility of public opinion, in part fuelled by the breakdown in the 'social contract', was left unspoken, but the result was acknowledged — "a climate in which the law must be seen against the background of other threats to workers' interests and trade union integrity."

Instead of the relatively rapid success in defeating and removing the legislation which the strategy required, the General Council more realistically expected that "the campaign to defeat this legislation is likely to be long and arduous." In terms of "industrial reality", therefore, it was not practicable to "lay down in advance a set response by the Movement to any situation which might emerge." Consequently, there was a "need for flexibility of tactics." Yet it was the very inflexibility of the 1971 strategy which had proved to be its strength. The refusal to register had placed the unions quite literally outside the law. Thus, while the movement was ostensibly committing itself to uncompromising opposition, the bolt-hole had already been prepared.

The TUC's 'New Realism'
The scale of Labour's defeat in the 1983 election undermined the

implicit assumptions of the Wembley strategy. Waiting for Labour and the repeal of the legislation now seemed like waiting for Godot; the unions were faced with the task of surviving in an inhospitable climate for an indefinite period ahead. At one level, the issue concerned the problematic posture towards the newly returned Thatcher Government. The decision at the September TUC conference to 'talk to Tebbit' represented more than the traditional ambition of the TUC to influence governments of whatever political persuasion. The TUC had refused to discuss the details of the Industrial Relations Bill once Employment Secretary Robert Carr ruled out negotiation over the central principles set out in his consultative document — the eight 'pillars' of the Bill. The decision to discuss the provisions of the proposed Trade Union Bill in an attempt to ameliorate the resultant legislation symbolised the acceptance by the TUC of the framework imposed by the Government. It was a complete reversal of the strategy agreed at Wembley. By seeking to mitigate the severity of the legislation the TUC was in fact mitigating the subsequent conflict and disruption when it came to be implemented, increasing the likelihood that the Act, and the Government's strategy as a whole, would be seen to 'work'.

The most dramatic manifestation of the TUC's reorientation towards the Government came with the request in December by the National Graphical Association (NGA) for TUC support in its action against the *Stockport Messenger*[7]. By repudiating on principle the decision of the Employment Policy and Organisation Committee to support the NGA's proposed national strike, TUC General Secretary Len Murray clearly aligned himself with the view that unions must always operate within the law. The endorsement of his action by a majority of the General Council, however, was more ambiguous; some members were motivated by purely tactical considerations — whether it was in fact possible for the TUC to deliver more than moral support and whether the NGA had a realistic strategy for winning the strike.

Considerations of this sort had been allowed to determine the response to conflicts arising under the Industrial Relations Act and were clearly consistent with the principles adopted at Wembley. Privately, Murray's handling of the issue was criticised for being unnecessarily divisive and for locking the TUC into a commitment which would weaken its bargaining position with the Government. The argument to the contrary that Murray had "put himself in a better position" to "win some success with this strategy in gaining concessions from the Government"[8] collapsed with the announcement by the Government a few weeks later of its decision to ban trade unions from Government Communications Headquarters (GCHQ) Cheltenham. For a time, 'New Realism' seemed to go into reverse as the TUC in a symbolic gesture withdrew its representatives from the National Economic Development Council (NEDC). However, the move at Congress to have this confirmed as a matter of principle failed and the ground was prepared for the return of the 'Neddy six'.

The fruit of the 'talks with Tebbit' and his successor Tom King over the Trade Union Bill was less equivocal. To avoid a threatened amendment to replace the system of individual 'contracting-out' of political funds by a requirement for 'contracting-in', the TUC issued in March 1984 a *Statement of Guidance* on the operation of the 'contracting-out' procedure. The Donovan Commission noted that: "When 'contracting-in' was substituted in 1927 for 'contracting-out' the result was to diminish very considerably the amount of money received by the trade unions' political funds." However, the price paid to avoid a possible recurrence of this was that the TUC had to take responsibility for policing a system which was not only unpopular with many union officials, but had also been opposed in principle at the time of its inception under the 1913 legislation on the ground that it ran counter to the normal collective decision-making processes of unions.

Thus, by the time the Trade Union Act reached the statute-book in July, there was no question of the TUC adopting a stance of non-compliance. Compliance with the requirements under Part I of the Act for election of union executives was left as a matter for individual unions, as was the issue of balloting before strikes. With the collapse of the strike at Austin-Rover in November 1984 and the failure of the attempt of the Transport and General Workers' Union (TGWU) to defy the courts following its fine for contempt, together with the ending of the miners' strike in March 1985, any prospect of serious resistance collapsed. NUR General Secretary Jimmy Knapp emerged as one of the strongest advocates of the balloting provisions, despite two damaging defeats and clear evidence of the difficulties caused to unions' attempts to resist closure programmes. Similarly, most unions apart from the Health Service Employees (COHSE) and the Local Government Officers (NALGO) have moved to bring their election procedures into line with the Act. In addition, the Trade Union Co-ordinating Committee was established in December 1984 to organise the political fund ballots campaign through to March 1986, in compliance with Part III of the Act.

Although TUC policy still opposed closed shop ballots, its underlying rationale had all but disappeared. Even before

November 1984 when the provisions of the 1982 Act came into effect, a number of unions at local or regional level had organised ballots to protect an existing arrangement where they believed they stood a good chance of winning the necessary majority. Similarly, the policy against acceptance of funds for balloting expenses came under increased pressure during 1985 as the Engineers (AEU) and the Electricians (EETPU) announced their intention to apply. In a shrewdly timed move, the Government provided in new regulations made in October 1984 that applications in respect of ballots held during 1984 would have to be made within six months of the regulations coming into force on 5th February 1985. The attempt to discipline the two unions resulted in the fiasco at the 1985 Congress and in April 1986 the General Council effectively dropped its opposition by permitting unions to decide the issue for themselves. Wembley had fallen apart. The danger this posed for the trade union movement had been highlighted at the 1985 Congress by Bill Keys, chairman of the TUC's Employment Policy Committee and of the Co-ordinating Committee for the political fund ballots. "Any modification to the policies which suggests a comfortable acceptance of the shackles that the Government have already placed upon us will make it unlikely that we shall ever be able to shake off the shackles."[9]

It would be wrong, however, to imply that such a result is inevitable. 'New realism' involved more than a simple ideological shift to the right to establish an accommodation with the Government over its labour law. At a deeper level, the pressures which had led the centre into this position were primarily industrial — the need to preserve and adapt organisation and bargaining structures which are the foundations of trade union power. Despite the battering received after 1979 and some well-publicised instances of a more aggressive management style, there is little evidence of a collapse of union influence at plant and company level[10].

The tension between the predominantly political and industrial orientations of 'new realism' surfaced in the comments made by the General, Municipal and Boilermakers' Union (GMBATU) on the *TUC Strategy* document launched in February 1984. Much of the latter was anodyne and uncontentious; but, on the whole, the tone was defensive and the primary concern appeared to be with "maintaining the political influence of the trade union movement in economic and social affairs" to offset the tendency for "technological change and the reduction in the demand for labour to continue to strengthen the employers' position..." In contrast, GMBATU maintained that independent organisation, not the benevolence of governments, was the foundation upon which trade union objectives could be secured — "the current bias of TUC activity towards...government...is a wrong sense of priorities in the current climate." Although a strategy of 'total opposition' might no longer be justifiable, "where necessary unions and the TUC must be prepared...to challenge the law, or to take industrial action on a political issue, which is itself potentially unlawful." This interplay between the political and industrial dimensions of 'new realism' has shaped the debate over new labour law, at least as regards its content. Its form reflected the influence of the parliamentary leadership of the Labour Party.

'Positive Rights' and 'Immunities'

In an interview with Labour's deputy leader Roy Hattersley in April 1985, 'Weekend World' presenter Brian Walden suggested that Labour may wish to reconsider its commitment to restore completely the trade union immunities. Referring to a discussion paper written by Labour's General Secretary Jim Mortimer, Walden put forward a possible alternative: "Labour could give the unions specific new rights to organise and take industrial action in a trade union Bill of Rights, but along with the legal rights would go legal obligations." Hattersley's response was non-committal beyond declaring an intention to discuss the matter with trade union leaders. However, an interview in *New Socialist*[11] gave an important clue to his thinking. Under the 'social contract', the Government had done things which it "believed to be undesirable" in return for union restraint on wages. In future, Hattersley suggested, "we have to look at the legal position on its own merits."

Ironically, Mortimer's paper, which had been approved by the Party's National Executive Committee (NEC) in January as a basis for further discussion on the Liaison Committee, was intended to forestall reconsiderations of the kind Hattersley was implying. For Mortimer, it was axiomatic that the unions should be restored at a minimum to the 1979 position and the Tory laws swept away entirely. The traditional method of protecting the right to take effective industrial action by means of 'immunities' was considered preferable to the introduction of new positive rights. Mortimer argued that a positive rights approach involved a number of problems. First, interpretation of rights would fall to the courts who would "come to see it as their duty to lay down the limits of these rights." Secondly, positive rights would invite further intervention into industrial relations by the courts and legislature. The result would be likely to "undermine the right of unions to conduct their own affairs."

On immunities, Mortimer's paper was consistent with the position taken by the TUC in its 1983 document *Repeal and Replacement Legislation* which considered that the traditional approach, "despite its drawback of appearing as a 'privilege'...has by and large served the trade union movement well." On ballots, however, Mortimer was prepared to go further than the TUC, proposing that the Trade Union Act 1913 should be repealed in addition to the Act of 1984, because the compromise on which it was based had been upset by the new legislation. It was "in principle always offensive because it represented the intervention of the State in the right of trade unions to determine their own policies."

Although Mortimer's paper set out for further discussion a range of possible changes in the law designed to enhance the rights of workers and trade unions, the predominant concern was to reduce the extent of intervention by the courts. Underlying the 'immunities' approach is the philosphy of 'voluntarism'. In 1968, Mortimer had proposed what for its time was a very ambitious programme of positive law reforms to extend trade union rights and the scope of employment protection[12]. However, the experience as Chairman of ACAS of operating the statutory recognition procedure under the Employment Protection Act 1975 was clearly a disillusioning one. In June 1979, Mortimer wrote to Tory Secretary of State Jim Prior advising him that the ACAS Council considered that it could not "satisfactorily operate the statutory recognition procedures as they stand", thus facilitating their repeal in the 1980 Employment Act. This experience is used as an illustration in the NEC paper of the case against positive rights and in favour of a voluntary approach generally. Indeed, Jim Mortimer has argued against the restoration of the 'general level' provisions in Schedule 11 of the 1975 Act, which entitled a union to bring a case against an employer paying less than the locally established going-rate for the job, on the grounds that there was "some strength in the employers' argument that this provision could operate as a ratchet for inflation"[13].

Throughout 1985, the debate surfaced in occasional remarks by leading figures in the labour movement linking the idea of 'positive rights' with the case for retaining some form of compulsory balloting provisions. The most important instance was at the press conference to launch the Liaison Committee document "A New Partnership: A New Britain"; this set out the "guiding principles" of Labour's approach — "involvement" and "fairness" — and promised to "repeal the present government's divisive trade union legislation and replace it with positive legislation." Enlarging upon this theme, Labour's leader Neil Kinnock stated that it would be "eccentric" for a movement pressing for more workers' rights to "mitigate these rights so far as their own organisations are concerned"[14].

At the Blackpool Congress in September 1985, the main composite motion on "Anti-trade union legislation" was drafted by the Transport and General Workers' Union from motions submitted by the TGWU, Civil Servants (CPSA), Train Drivers (ASLEF), Print Workers (SOGAT) and Technical Staff (TASS). The CPSA motion calling for a "Review of current industrial legislation" by the Liaison Committee stated explicitly that the purpose should be to "see which parts require repeal to safeguard the future effective role of the trade union Movement and which parts could be tolerated, or amended in such a way that they will be acceptable to the trade union Movement." This passage was deleted from the composite which therefore expressed the position of the TGWU — seeking a commitment from the Labour Party to repeal all the Tory legislation in the first session of a Labour Government and confirming "the policy of non-co-operation agreed at the Special TUC Conference at Wembley in 1982." A motion from the EETPU that the Wembley decisions "were dependent upon the election of a Labour Government at the subsequent General Election", which more accurately reflected the real balance of forces, was voted down. The formal victory of the TGWU, however, merely provided a smokescreen behind which those forces could safely manoeuvre to undermine it.

TUC General Secretary Norman Willis had on a number of occasions signalled his willingness to retain some form of balloting provision, at least if this was coupled with improved workplace facilities for unions to hold meetings and organise. Many of the right-wing unions, most importantly the AEU and the EETPU, were also prepared to accept compulsory pre-strike ballots. But there was a complicating factor. The parliamentary leadership were pressing for a shift to a 'positive framework' of law in the belief that politically this would facilitate the 'balance of rights and responsibilities' they wanted to create. Ballots could be justified in terms of the rights of individual members and the responsibilities of unions to them and the public at large. It would also allow them to honour the commitment to repeal the Tory legislation before re-enacting it in a new form. However, the TUC was still committed by tradition and policy to the immunities approach. Similarly, both the AEU and the EETPU, whose craft tradition sustained an essentially 'voluntarist' outlook, were hostile to a shift towards the more interventionist approach symbolised by the notion of 'positive rights'.

Cross Currents and Confusion
In December 1985, the AEU General Secretary Gavin Laird attacked the proposed replacement of the immunities by a system of positive rights. Extending legal protection to workers regardless of trade union membership could lead to a rapid decline in trade unionism, he argued. "What those in the trade union movement who advocate such a bill of rights are, in effect, arguing for is the rapid development of the conditions in which workers feel that they do not need to belong to a trade union."[15] In other words, there was no direct correlation between the substantive debate over ballots and the position on positive rights. The old argument on 'voluntarism' cut across the newer split over ballots; the 'immunities' camp was divided into a left-wing, whose position was articulated by Mortimer, and the right-wing of Laird. The right-wing supporters of compulsory ballots were themselves divided between those whose orientation was primarily political — towards the Labour leadership who favoured positive rights — and on the other hand, the traditional industrial right-wing supporters of 'voluntarism'.

The lack of an apparent correlation between the debate over 'positive rights' and 'immunities' and the ballots issue undoubtedly created considerable confusion. Lord McCarthy's Fabian Society pamphlet, *Freedom at Work: Towards the Reform of Tory Employment Laws* (November, 1985), sought to resolve some of the conflicts by providing a detailed set of reform proposals. In general terms, there were two main objectives. First, a distinction was drawn between the political presentation of Labour's policies and their enactment as legislation. In McCarthy's view, "Labour should present its proposed alternative framework in similarly (i.e. to other European Community countries) positive terms, avoiding the negative language of immunities..." However, such a change in political presentation "should not be taken to the point where it pre-judges and predetermines the ultimate language to be used in a future statute." It was "essential to hang onto the point that by speaking the language of rights we do not actually solve any of the major problems." In other words, trade unions could allow the Party to talk about 'positive rights' without committing themselves to any particular legislative content.

Secondly, there was to be a much greater emphasis on union ballots as a condition for the exercise of rights and freedoms. In fact, this point flows directly from the supposedly "largely presentational...case for focusing on the rights and freedoms of individual workers, rather than the immunities of their unions. This approach has implications for the right of members to be consulted and to decide things for themselves..." (p.21). Hence, the operation of the watered-down closed shop McCarthy advocated would be dependent on majority support in a ballot; the right "to present a wage claim and have it taken seriously" would depend upon at least 30 per cent support in the bargaining unit and majority support would be necessary to present a claim to "binding arbitration." On the 1984 Act, Part III dealing with political funds should be retained and a similar provision extended to "corporate bodies of all kinds". Part I on election of union executives is unnecessarily rigid, for example, in its exclusion of indirect election. McCarthy seemed to suggest its replacement by a more flexible Code of Practice, which would nevertheless have some statutory backing as a standard "in deciding how far individual unions were entitled to enforce their new rights."

In the Fabian pamphlet, McCarthy argued against retention of compulsory pre-strike ballots. In his experience, "properly conducted meetings at the place of work can be an equally valid way of deciding whether or not to use industrial action." These should be "encouraged and facilitated" through the provision of adequate time-off and other arrangements to enable all workers to attend and become involved in discussion. The positions on Parts I and II of the Act, however, were soon overtaken by events. At a Fabian Society meeting in March 1986, where McCarthy debated with Jim Mortimer, he shifted his ground of objection to Part II — employers should not have any right to enforce the balloting requirements. Indirect election of union executives should be allowed; but there should be a set of statutory minimum rule book standards enforceable by individual members in industrial tribunals. Perhaps these shifts in position may to some extent be accounted for by the increasing support within the trade unions for the principle of compulsory ballots.

The responses to the TUC's consultative document on *Industrial Relations Legislation* submitted by unions for the conference on 19th March 1986 demonstrated the various cross currents[16]. A significant minority favoured retention of compulsory strike ballots, but were divided on the issue of 'immunities' — the AEU, EETPU, and Equity were in favour, while the Institute for Professional Civil Servants (IPCS), SOGAT, the Communication Workers (UCW), and CPSA preferred 'positive rights'. Of those opposed to statutory provisions, the TGWU, NALGO, and COHSE wanted to retain 'immunities', while the Mineworkers (NUM), TASS, and the Society of Civil and Public Servants (SCPS) wanted a positive right to strike, or a mixture of rights and immunities. The National Union of Public Employees (NUPE) seemed inclined towards 'immunities' without ruling out positive rights, as were GMBATU and the Cinema and Television Technicians (ACTT). NUPE was against legally compulsory balloting; GMBATU did not take a definite position on this issue, but did insist that ballots could only be contemplated in the form of a right for union members and not, as the 1984 Act provided, a legal weapon in the hands of employers. This was also the position of the TUC: "If a Labour Government's policy was to encourage strike ballots in some form or other, enforcement of members' rights in this respect should not be linked to the lawfulness *per se* of the industrial action concerned (injunctions, damages, etc.) but should take the form of union members making a complaint...which if upheld might result in an order simply requiring that a ballot should now be held" (5.14).

Superficially, the unions appeared prepared to accommodate the Labour leaders on ballots to a very considerable extent. However, the 'positive rights' strategy designed to facilitate this now proved to be a source of difficulty. First, there was the opposition of the AEU and EETPU. The views of a number of unions on the 'immunities' issue demonstrated little recognition of any point of political principle or interest to them; consequently, they were shallow and of little weight. Both the AEU and the EETPU, however, were prepared for their own reasons to accept compulsory ballots while positively rejecting the idea of more positive rights.

Secondly, other unions from the opposite standpoint were demanding more in the way of positive rights than was set out in the TUC's Consultative Document. This addressed itself mainly to the question spelt out in the original CPSA motion to Congress — what parts of the Tory legislation should be retained or modified rather than repealed? In their submissions to the TUC, both NALGO and the SCPS suggested that this focus reflected excessively the interests of the Labour Party. NUPE pointed out that "the TUC has not attempted to identify broad aims or principles which might guide our reforms of industrial relations law" and argued for more emphasis on "strong collective organisation", on "strengthening workers' rights", and on such issues as fair wages and industrial democracy. GMBATU agreed that "new industrial relations laws must be part of a coherent programme of social and economic reform." The treatment of employment protection laws in particular — left by the TUC to an "incoming Labour Government to mount a major review" — and of anti-discrimination law was considered to be "disgraceful".

Thirdly, the 'positive rights' approach had resulted in the acceptance of compulsory ballots only in a particular restricted form. It seems that the strategy was originally conceived as a means of securing the acceptance of duties or 'responsibilities' to 'balance' or, more accurately, restrict the exercise of the right. For example, the Irish proposals[17] envisage a positive right to strike which would be restricted in much the same way as the immunities under the 1980 Employment Act. It would also permit employers to obtain an injunction where the union had not won a majority in a secret ballot or had failed to give proper notice. Most unions, however, interpreted the linking of positive rights with ballots to mean that only individual union members would be able to enforce the right, not employers or other parties affected by any industrial action. These difficulties were to exert a profound influence over the process of drafting the final document.

The Drafting Process: Conflict and Agreement

Following the conference at Congress House, a paper was prepared by the Labour Party for the Liaison Committee putting the case for a positive right to strike[18]. It had two main objectives. First, consistently with the position of the TUC and most unions, it separated the question of strike ballots from the right to strike. On the surface, this may appear little more than a legalistic quibble over whether unions should be taken to court by employers or their own members. After all, many of the most damaging legal actions, from the Osborne judgment to the cases against the NUM, have been brought by union members.In symbolic political terms, however, the distinction is of fundamental significance. While it leaves open the possibility that 'positive rights' could be used as a means of providing rights to individual workers inconsistent with independent collective organisation, it excludes the idea of 'balancing' rights with 'responsibilities'. From this latter standpoint, conferring a positive right to strike without, at the same time, qualifying it with restrictions such as the duty to hold a ballot undermines the main purpose behind the shift from the system of 'immunities'.

The second objective of the paper was to demonstrate that a 'positive rights' approach could be used consistently with the principles of collective organisation to strengthen the position of unions compared with the 'immunities' provided under the last

Labour Government. In addition to providing more comprehensive protection against the courts in cases of industrial action, including picketing, workers should be protected against dismissal for taking industrial action and should also enjoy the normal rights to social security payments. In other words, the paper sought to establish a 'left' position within the 'positive rights' camp — a stronger right to strike, legal support for collective bargaining, and strengthened employment protection. The balance of power, however, was held by the 'centre' who, in return for positive measures of this kind, were prepared to accommodate the 'right' on compulsory ballots — not as a 'responsibility' balancing a positive right to strike, but as a distinct right for individual workers. For the 'centre', balloting was not acceptable as a restriction on the right to strike but only as a concession made in return for other 'positive rights' such as industrial democracy and employment protection. The principle of "workers' rights" sustained a different conception of the "balanced framework of law", guaranteeing (in theory if not necessarily in reality) most of the positive measures sought by the unions.

The decision to discuss first a document dealing solely with the right to strike, rather than a full draft of the intended final statement, effectively squeezed out the 'centre'. The only way such a document could achieve 'balance' was to make balloting a condition of the right to strike. Instead, an unlimited right to strike was proposed by playing-off the known position of the 'centre' against the 'right', without making any commitment at all on the question of compulsory pre-strike ballots. On the morning of the Liaison Committee meeting, the document was described on the front page of the *Financial Times* under the headline: "Unlimited right to strike urged.". This set the stage for it to be thrown out; according to reports[19], Labour leader Neil Kinnock argued, with the support of the TUC General Secretary and the leader of the Scientific and Managerial Union (ASTMS), Clive Jenkins, that the document failed absolutely to strike the proper "balance of rights and responsibility" because it did not begin from the necessity of ballots. In the circumstances, perhaps it is less surprising that the paper was not accepted than that it was even discussed. Normally, meetings of the committee are not called to throw out a document rather than amend it, since the objective is to produce an agreed statement. This in itself testifies to the tangled communications produced by the Byzantine back-stage manoeuvring.

The only way to break the impasse over the right to strike was to place this particular issue back into the context of industrial relations policy as a whole, to deal with the question of ballots. But the 'centre' would only deal with ballots in the context of "workers' rights" as a whole. The TUC originally was prepared to leave this area until another occasion — on industrial democracy it was merely noted that "work is also proceeding", while employment protection was to be left to an "incoming Labour Government". The alignment of forces now enabled a major shift of ground to take place; the pivotal position was occupied by John Edmonds, general secretary of GMBATU.

On the eve of taking office from David Basnett, for some years the 'centre of gravity' on the General Council, Edmonds issued a major statement calling for a change in outlook on the part of the unions, with more emphasis being given to the interests of working people as a whole, particularly those in the highly fragmented service sectors where pay and conditions were worst. He developed the theme at an industrial relations conference in March[20], arguing for an "ambitious package" of law reforms covering such matters as unfair dismissal, redundancy procedures and payments, minimum conditions of employment, health and safety, and especially equal opportunities — which GMBATU's submission to the TUC stated "should be the corner-stone of our campaign — regaining support from women and minorities."

Although the GMBATU has eschewed "long academic debates about legal principles"[21], this approach epitomises a central strand of the centre-left 'positive rights' strategy. Edmonds has adapted the strategy to the current political climate by presenting it in terms of "individual rights" and an opportunity for the trade unions to establish a "broader appeal". There is danger, however, pointed out recently by Jim Mortimer[22], of giving the impression that "individual rights are seen as an alternative to the full protection of collective trade union rights", or that "emphasis is being placed on individual rights because it might be more difficult to argue for collective rights."

Nevertheless, despite the rhetorical gloss, the policy is firmly based on GMBATU's interest in organising these workers, who, without some degree of legal protection, do not possess sufficient strength to sustain collective organisation in the face of hostility from the employers. For example, in the Grosvenor Hotel dispute in 1983, trade union members were sacked with impunity when they were held by the courts to fall outside outside the scope of the unfair dismissal law[23]. Fundamentally, the different views on employment law espoused by GMBATU and the EETPU reflect a difference in organising strategy which itself is due to the respective strength or weakness in the labour market of the workers they are seeking to attract.

Paradoxically, then, the effect of the emphasis on ballots was to produce a shift, via the notion of "workers' rights", towards giving much greater weight than originally intended to employment protection and industrial democracy. A number of other factors worked in the same direction. First, the use of the 'democratic' principle to justify legislation on balloting in unions made it difficult to resist the argument that this should also be applied consistently to employers — not in the form of ballots, but by developing the already agreed policy on industrial democracy. Secondly, the argument linking rights with responsibilities — intended as a means of restricting the rights — could be used in a different sense to justify the extension of workers' influence as the condition for their acceptance of greater responsibility. Thirdly, the themes of 'involvement', 'freedom' and 'fairness', already given political currency, could be easily adapted to promote rights for "People at Work". The influence of these principles and themes can be seen at a glance in the document's list of "Contents"[24].

Strikes and Ballots

It is not proposed here to embark on a detailed critical analysis of the various proposals and gaps in the final document, or to suggest ways in which it could be 'improved', an undertaking which depends obviously on the political standpoint of the critic. It is not a blueprint for future legislation. Many issues or problems are avoided or 'fudged' — capable of bearing different interpretations. Compromises have not been worked through in sufficient detail to see whether they are genuinely practicable or illusory. The significance of the document lies in its expression of the various currents at work within the labour movement, of the way in which they interact in this area of policy, and of possible future developments. What remains for present purposes is to trace the implications of the debate on the issues constituting the original point of departure.

The 'positive rights' strategy was launched as a vehicle to retain the substance of the Tory legislation in a new form. It was undermined and rendered superfluous by the opposition of the AEU and EETPU, who were prepared to accept the 1984 Trade Union Act in substantially its present form, as part of a system of immunities. The compromise formula which emerged from the TUC conference in March 1986 — a "combination of rights and immunities" — was intended merely to end the debate harmlessly, but was given a definite legal and political content in the *Right to Strike* paper for the Liaison Committee. In contrast, the formula which appears in the final document — "a mixture of rights, immunities and responsibilities" — is an empty phrase designed to satisfy all parties but devoid of concrete content.

The scope for legitimate industrial action is expanded "to reflect the wider collective bargaining agenda envisaged in our proposals on industrial democracy"; but, by implication, it appears to be restricted to disputes with employers, thus excluding action taken to pressure a government. The single sentence on picketing does not deal with problems such as the stopping of vehicles — it contains no specific commitments; the power to grant injunctions preventing industrial action will remain. The most significant proposal in this section of the document therefore is to establish "a new tripartite body, comparable perhaps to the Central Arbitration Committee" — to give a preliminary ruling in cases challenging the validity of industrial action — or, alternatively "a specialist court".

The Donovan Commission very carefully distinguished between its proposals to extend the jurisdiction of the industrial tribunals and the "labour courts" which exist in a number of EEC countries, a point of great sensitivity to the TUC. "We do not propose that they should be given the job of resolving industrial disputes...Nor do we envisage that any matters arising between trade unions and their members or applicants for membership should be within the jurisdiction of the labour tribunals..."[25]. One of the principal trade union objections to the Industrial Relations Act was its creation of a special labour court designed to 'victimise' trade unions; hence, the Tory legislation after 1980 was designed to be administered through the ordinary courts. Possibly this has contributed to the radical change in thinking on this issue, but more fundamentally, it reflects the weakening of the 'voluntarist' sentiment which provided the main ideological attack on the 1971 Act. *People at Work* states that there is "no question of excluding the law from industrial relations" (para.8).

Paradoxically, however, this trends appears to be reinforced by a sentiment derived from the voluntarist tradition — the desire to keep "the courts" out of industrial relations. Rationally, this means the same as keeping "the law" out of industrial relations — avoiding the imposition of legal sanctions. But it also carries with it a special element of antipathy towards the judges and the ordinary courts who have developed the common law and interpreted statutory law in a manner hostile to unions. There is a hope that a special labour court, less 'ignorant' of industrial relations, might be favourably disposed towards the unions. Almost certainly, this is wishful thinking[26]. What such a court would do is to legitimise and facilitate greater legal controls and restrictions over collective bargaining, including ultimately the legal enforcement of collective agreements, and over internal trade union procedures. A similar suggestion in an early draft of the 1983 TUC document on *Repeal and Replacement Legislation* was rapidly thrown out after appearing on the front page of the *Financial Times*. Its survival in the present document is linked to the position on balloting.

There were a number of possible options on balloting, from returning the law to the position before the 1984 Act at one end to retaining it unaltered at the other. Both these 'extreme' options were rejected on the ground that, while something had to be done about ballots, the present law was "unacceptably wide". In May 1986, the Liaison Committee rejected a first draft option to establish statutory provisions governing union elections and strike ballots, with the main opposition coming from the TGWU. That left a choice between two further possibilities. The TUC could issue a code of practice on balloting and perhaps a set of loosely drawn 'model rules'; complaints about balloting irregularities could be taken by union members to the TUC Independent Review Committee. Extending the jurisdiction of the Committee in this way could also be used to justify excluding the powers of the ordinary courts to intervene in trade union procedures through enforcement of the rule book, thus providing protection from the kind of actions, including appointment of a receiver, which had crippled the NUM during its strike. The intention of the 1871 Trade Union Act could be re-established.

The third option was to create a statutory requirement on unions to adopt suitable rules providing for individual balloting over strikes and for executive elections. By the June meeting, the TGWU had been persuaded to withdraw its opposition to the principle of statutory enforcement. The wording agreed proposed "laying down statutory principles for inclusion in union rule books". The reference to rule books appeared consistent with the third option, but it was in substance identical to the first option rejected in May — the requirements were to be prescribed in law, with no discretion left to individual unions.

In mid-July, NALGO launched a public attack on the balloting proposals as an infringement of ILO Convention No.87, Article 3, protecting the right of unions to draw up their own constitutions and rules and restraining the public authorities from any interference which would restrict this freedom. Legally speaking, the argument had a degree of plausibility, but the ILO principles do not provide absolute guarantees of trade union freedoms. In practice, they are conveniently interpreted subject to the political conceptions of the Western 'liberal democracies'. For example, legislation "intended to promote democratic principles within trade union organisation" is acceptable[27]. In 1985, the ILO Committee of Experts rejected a complaint from the TUC that the 1984 Act infringed the Convention.

Politically speaking, however, the attack was very effective. The ILO Conventions establish only minimum conditions for the operation of independent trade unionism. For the TUC to be forced to defend its own policy in public against a charge of infringing the Convention was a humiliation. It was also highly embarrassing to have the arguments the TUC had used against the Tory legislation turned around, and to cite the rejection of its own complaint by the Committee of Experts as an authority against the argument of NALGO.

The principle on which the TUC had relied in its original complaint was that: "Legislation which regulates in detail the internal election procedures of trade unions is incompatible with the rights of trade unions recognised by Convention No.87" Advancing the same argument against the TUC-Labour Party draft reinforced the pressure to further relax the proposed requirements. At a meeting of Labour's National Executive, a motion proposed by NUPE deputy general secretary Tom Sawyer was passed, altering the wording of the draft by substituting "general principles" for "statutory" ones. A counter-move by Neil Kinnock re-inserted "statutory" at a different point, so that the final proposal reads: "This new statutory framework will also entail laying down general principles for inclusion in trade union rule books etc ". The effect of these changes was to move away from the first option set out above towards the third.[28]

The second point of contention debated by the NEC concerned the mechanism of enforcement. There are several possibilities here — the ordinary courts, a special labour court, the certification officer, the industrial tribunals, or a non-statutory body such as the Independent Review Committee — each having different implications for procedures and appropriate sanctions. The draft before the NEC proposed a "new independent tribunal" which "would adopt a conciliatory and flexible approach", although ultimately it would be "empowered to require a union to...remedy the complaint." Only after the procedures of the tribunal were exhausted would it be possible to take the complaint to the ordinary courts.

The idea behind this proposal is similar to that for a "new tripartite body" which would make a preliminary ruling on applications for labour injunctions. The fact that the jurisdiction for ordinary courts is not excluded altogether, but merely suspended temporarily, seems to imply that these bodies would not wield the powers of a court. They seem designed to act as a kind of insulating layer between the law and its ultimate enforcement by the courts. However, the political logic behind such a labour tribunal is that it would probably evolve into a specialist court. Ironically, an amendment approved by the NEC designed to exclude more effectively the ordinary courts, providing that they would only hear appeals on a point of law, has given further impetus in this direction. It would still be possible to keep separate the body making a final decision on the complaint from the enforcement of that decision by an ordinary court, as with arbitration awards made by the Central Arbitration Committee under its statutory jurisdiction, although it is difficult to see more than a possible presentational advantage.

Considering the complex, accident-prone nature of the drafting process, it is scarcely surprising that the meeting of the Liaison Committee in July to approve the final version was cancelled. Having been approved by the NEC, it was then passed by the General Council with representatives from NALGO, NUPE, COHSE, TASS, and the NUM voting against, reflecting the official position of those unions, together with some other members.

Will Labour Repeal the Tory Union Laws?

The emphasis on 'individual rights' in the document, linking the sections on positive workers' rights with ballots, indicates the supremacy of the position described here as the 'centre'. The clearest and most coherent parts are those dealing with the themes of involvement in change and "fairness and job security" — the bulk of the document. The few paragraphs dealing with statutory requirements for balloting and the nature of the tribunal to enforce them are in "so verbose and garbled a form that it is difficult for any voter to make out Labour's policy on these two points."[29] However, the 'centre' position in this context involves a contradiction between two different kinds of rights and two different strategies.

Rights given to workers against employers can be consistent with collective organisation since the objectives are the same; in contrast, rights given to workers individually against trade unions weaken the position of workers against the employer by constricting the freedom of collective organisation. The nature of any 'individual right' depends upon the direction in which it runs in the power relationship between worker and employer. On balloting, the issue is not whether ballots are, in the abstract, a good thing, but how the law encourages their use. There might be an obligation on employers to provide facilities for the conduct of workplace ballots, leaving unions free to decide when to have them; alternatively, they can be imposed upon unions by force of law. Another approach could be to make entitlement to certain positive rights, such as protection against dismissal for taking industrial action, dependent upon a ballot[30]. The purpose of the Tory legislation, despite the "fancy theories" on democracy, is not to give individual workers greater influence over decisions affecting their working lives, but to "clip the wings of the trade unions and weaken their bargaining power", according to Ford's Director of Industrial Relations[31].

The provisions in the Labour-TUC document on balloting run directly counter to those designed to strengthen workers against employers. The acceptance of compulsory ballots by the trade unions, under pressure from the Labour Party leaders, is an unprecedented turn-round in relations between the Party and the unions.

It marks the profound transformation in the political climate which has occurred since the battle over *In Place of Strife* in 1969. To have rejected the demands on ballots would have entailed not only a repudiation of the Labour leaders themselves, but of their whole political line. What, then, are the implications of this line for industrial relations policy as a whole? Are ballots a separate issue, on which a tactical concession can be made without threatening other parts of the programme, or are they merely the 'thin end of the wedge', leading inexorably to more or less wholesale retention of the Tory legislation?

The collapse of the positive rights strategy to re-enact parts of the Tory legislation in a different form means that the existing legislation will probably not be repealed. The real significance of the provisions on balloting in *People at Work*, whatever the tortured compromises it contains, will be to allow a future Labour Government to retain the 1984 Act, pending a detailed examination of possible changes. This was the approach used by the Hawke Labour Government in Australia, with the result that legislation against secondary boycotts introduced in 1977 remains in force.

If this trend remains dominant, there will be no short repeal measure giving the unions an opportunity to filibuster over replacement legislation — the balloting provisions are not a mere pre-election gimmick designed to deceive the electorate, although it seems some union leaders have deceived themselves here. Leaving the 1984 Act in force would also affect the 1980 and 1982 Acts with which it is connected in various ways, politically and legally. It does not mean necessarily that no parts of the legislation will be repealed or amended, but the 'step by step' approach to repeal and replacement advocated by Lord McCarthy[32] implies that much, perhaps the greater part, will stay. The statement in *People at Work* that employers will be fully involved in these discussions to "demonstrate our determination to proceed by agreement as far as possible" (para.74) gives little cause for thinking otherwise. It is one thing to involve employers in matters where, in any event, they have the final word, but another to expect them to acquiesce easily in proposals to remove restrictions from trade unions and promote collective bargaining as a method of making their decisions "accountable to workers and society" (para.49).

Ultimately, however, there is a limit to how much light can be shed on the implications of any step or proposal by scrutinising documents or guessing at the real intentions of the Labour leaders. The decisive factors are power and the kind of relationship between trade unions and the state. The failure of the Wembley confrontation strategy to inflict serious damage on the Tory industrial relations policy has left the legislation intact as an effective package of measures to restrict trade union power. The exercise of trade union power has, in the past, caused considerable difficulty to Labour governments pursuing strategies requiring the containment of that power. A future Labour Government concerned primarily with the reduction of unemployment might view a possible revival of trade union power in more favourable economic circumstances with some degree of apprehension. In what circumstances, then, would such a Government have an interest in removing an effective set of constraints from the unions and replacing it with measures designed positively to enhance their influence?

The issue here concerns incomes policy[33]. In the past, incomes policy has curbed the use of bargaining power without attacking at its roots. The collapse of the 'social contract' marked the close of this phase. Incomes policy may possibly be seen as an alternative to 'monetarism', but no longer as an alternative to a restrictive industrial relations policy; the wholesale removal of legal restrictions is unlikely to occur until the unions can use their power more constructively as part of a new economic and industrial policy. Industrial democracy therefore provides the key to the future course of labour law.

People at Work contains two different strategies reflecting different problems and approaches, and attempts to find a compromise between them: on the one hand, the tendency to accommodate to the present political climate, which is strongest within the Party, but also exists within the unions to the extent that they have either adapted to it industrially like the EETPU or desire the election of a Labour Government; on the other hand, the struggle of the labour movement, fuelled by the industrial interests of most workers and trade unions, to shift onto more favourable terrain.

References

1. *One Step Forward, Two Steps Back* (1904)
2. N. Kinnock, *The Future of Socialism* (Fabian Society, 1985) pp.2-3.
3. See Chapter 4.
4. "People at Work: New Rights, New Responsibilities"; "Low Pay: Policies and Priorities", TUC-Labour Party, (July 1986).
5. See Green and Wilson, "The Future Course of Planning" in Topham (ed) *Planning the Planners*, Spokesman (1983).
6. Or, alternatively, 80 per cent of those entitled to vote, as under the 1980 Act. The 1982 Act's provisions came into force in November, 1984. From that date, any dismissal in a closed shop which has not been approved in a secret ballot is unfair.
7. See Gennard, "The Implications of the Messenger Newspaper Group Dispute" *Industrial Relations Journal* Vol 15/3, 1984.
9. TUC Report 1985, p.435.
10. See E. Batstone, *Working Order* (1984); *Union Structure and Strategy in the Face of Technical Change* (1985).
11. *New Socialist*, June 1985
12. Mortimer and Jenkins, *The Kind of Laws the Unions Ought to Want* (1968) esp. pp.52-6 on a positive right to recognition.
13. "Arbitration, the Public Interest and Labour Relations" in Wedderburn and Murphy (eds) *Labour Law and the Community* (1982) p.65
14. "Kinnock hints at retention of ballot law", *Financial Times* 7.8.85.
15. *Financial Times*, 31.12.85.
16. See "The Future of Labour Law: Positive Rights and Immunities" (1986) *The Industrial Tutor*.
17. "Outline of Principal Provisions of Proposed New Trade Dispute and Industrial Relations Legislation" (Dept. of Labour, Jan. 1986).
18. *op.cit.* ref. 16
19. *Guardian, Financial Times*, March 25, 1986.
20. *Warwick Papers in Industrial Relations*, 1986; *New Socialist*, June 1986 (see Chapter 8).
21. GMBATU, *Fair Laws and Rights in Employment* (1986) p.2
22. See Chapter 5.
23. O'Kelly v Trusthouse Forte (1983) *Industrial Relations Law Reports* 369.
24. See Chapter 3.
25. *Donovan Report* (1968) para. 576; TUC, *Action on Donovan*, para. 71.
26. Kahn-Freund, "The Social Ideal of the Reich Labour Court" (1931) in Lewis and Clark (eds) *Labour Law and Politics in the Weimar Republic* (1981).
27. *General Survey on Freedom of Association and Collective Bargaining* (1983) para. 169.
28. Since the document does not specify that a ballot should be held before a strike commences, unions could obtain some advantage from a delayed

timing of the ballot.
29. *The Economist*, July 26, 1986.
30. An amendment including a proposal to this effect moved by NALGO at a meeting on July 16 of the TUC's Employment Policy Committee was rejected.
31. Paul Roots, *Warwick Papers in Industrial Relations* No. 5
32. *Freedom at Work*, p.9
33. "Low Pay: Policies and Priorities", paras. 56, 93-100.

Chapter 3

Freedom and Fairness at Work
Roy Green

Freedom and fairness will be the unifying themes of a new partnership between the next Labour Government and ordinary trade union members. That is the consistent message of a series of economic policy statements drawn up in the TUC-Labour Party Liaison Committee, the forum which brings together leading figures from the Party's National Executive, Shadow Cabinet and TUC General Council.

Last year's statement, *A New Partnership: A New Britain*, welded these themes into a new 'vision' of Britain as "a more accountable and democratic economy" and as "a fairer society". It suggested that the aim of a high investment, high productivity, high wage economy could only be achieved "if we work together and draw upon all our resources, especially the talent and enthusiasm of working people themselves".

As a prerequisite, Labour would repeal the present government's trade union legislation and replace it with "positive legislation". Although the form of this legislation was not spelt out, the broad thrust was clear.

There would be new rights for workers to develop a comprehensive "strategy for fair wages" and, in addition, "to widen the collective bargaining agenda beyond wages to crucial investment decisions". These rights were seen as "a catalyst for the extension of democratic involvement and accountability not just within the enterprise but also beyond it in sector and national planning" (see also Prescott, 1985).

The New Statements
This year's TUC-Labour Party statements for the first time spell out in some detail the twin themes of "freedom and fairness for people at work". They begin from the premise that, "all workers

should be entitled to job security and a fair wage. And they should be given the chance to play a constructive and responsible role in the decisions which affect them".

A major statement on industrial relations, *People at Work: New Rights, New Responsibilities*, covers the whole field of workers' rights and industrial democracy. A further statement, *Low Pay: Policies and Priorities*, sets out the main elements of a fair wages strategy with particular emphasis on a national minimum wage.

This chapter will focus on the industrial democracy proposals of *People at Work* and their implications for the future direction of Labour's economic strategy. Just as this Government's trade union legislation has become "a centrepiece of its whole approach to economic strategy", so the role of the law in a positive counter-strategy must be "to enlarge, not diminish, the freedom of workers to control their environment".

No Going Back

The origins of *People at Work* are important. They lie not just in the traditional industrial relations concerns of the TUC but also in the Party's perception of its electoral interests and priorities. Despite a firm commitment to repeal the 1980 and 1982 Employment Acts and 1984 Trade Union Act, there is a widespread recognition that it will not be possible or even desirable for the next Labour Government just to restore the previous position.

Some observers have interpreted this shift in approach to mean that, "Labour would retain more of the existing legal framework than might appear likely from past declarations" (B.C.Roberts, *Financial Times*, 16th July, 1986). That may be the case — or it may not. Neither conclusion follows automatically from the demand for fresh legislation.

One fact is certain. The 1970s legislation provided inadequate protection for unions and their members. In particular, the 'immunity' afforded to industrial action was limited by the definition of a 'trade dispute', which was interpreted more and more narrowly by judges. For example, action concerning issues which come within the managerial prerogative were found to be unlawful, as were so-called 'political' strikes over privatisation and South Africa.

Yet it is the dispute at Wapping which has highlighted in the most dramatic fashion a raft of defects in the law which are unrelated to the legislation of the 1980s. This dispute, along with the banning of unions at the Government Communications Headquarters (GCHQ), has also contributed to a marked change in the public mood. Whereas restrictive union legislation may be 'popular' in the abstract, the behaviour of an archetypal Thatcherite employer has provoked genuine revulsion.

Positive Rights
The proposal for a 'positive right' to strike was advanced not as an alternative to immunities but to expand the scope for industrial action by removing the need to define a 'trade dispute'. Instead of protecting the *purpose* for which action was taken, a positive legal right would afford clear protection to the *action itself*, i.e. a strike or other legitimate form of industrial action.

Moreover, an approach based on positive rights would confer a significant political advantage (McCarthy, 1985). Whereas immunities can be presented as 'privileges' which place unions 'above the law', a right to strike is generally accepted as a basic civil liberty in a democratic society. This was demonstrated recently in Germany where the trade union movement succeeded in mobilising huge opposition to the Kohl Government's threatened erosion of the right to strike.

Ironically, it is the European example which has fuelled union suspicion of positive rights. There is justifiable concern, especially in the light of the widely circulated Irish Ministry of Labour proposals, that legal rights will bring in their wake restrictive obligations — perhaps enforceable in a new system of labour courts. This concern was strongly expressed in many union responses to the TUC's major consultative document, *Industrial Relations Legislation* (January 1986).

And Immunities
Of course, no union goes out of its way to promote strikes or disruption — the well-being of its members is usually best served by joint negotiation and agreement at the workplace. Indeed, most unions will take elaborate steps to avoid strikes if they can, exploring the possibilities for settlement through conciliation bodies such as the Advisory, Conciliation and Arbitration Service (ACAS). Ultimately, however, employees must retain the freedom to withdraw their labour and take collective action without fear of prosecution.

While it is not within the scope of this article to consider in detail how this freedom might be secured in law, union responses to the TUC consultation did point to an emerging consensus. This would *combine* a new positive right to strike with a modified form of immunity from legal liabilities, designed to protect workers from injunctions and damages inflicted by the courts. It is this consensus which is embodied — separately from union balloting requirements — in *People at Work* (see the discussion in *Tribune*, 7th & 21st June, 5th July, 1985; 18th April, 1986).

Fair Treatment

A further reason for not going back to the pre-1979 position may be found in the labour market itself. The pattern of work in Britain has been changing rapidly, leading to the growth of what GMBATU General Secretary, John Edmonds, calls a 'new exploited class' of part-time, temporary and casual labour.

The vast majority are women, who, through a variety of circumstances, tend to get trapped in low paid, low status jobs. These are jobs where there is often little experience of trade union organisation, and where rights to fair wages and employment security have either been stripped away by the Government or never existed at all.

The *People at Work* statement rejects the Government's "pretext of reducing 'burdens' on employers". Under the general heading of 'fairness and job security', it proposes new legislation which would for the first time give 'employee status' to part-time and temporary workers, including homeworkers.

This radical reform would entitle these as well as other workers to expanded rights covering redundancies, training, unfair dismissal, equal opportunities, health and safety, and low pay. Such rights are necessary not as a substitute for collective bargaining and organisation but to assist trade unions in overcoming the weakness of the most isolated and vulnerable groups (Hepple, 1986).

Democracy

Legislation directly promoting the freedom of employees to organise in unions and bargain with their employer is dealt with in the statement under the heading of 'involvement in change'. Moreover, industrial democracy, instead of being treated separately as in the past, is now seen as an integral part of the broad extension of workers' rights.

A previous TUC-Labour Party statement, *Economic Planning and Industrial Democracy* (1982), took an important step in linking workers' involvement with the processes of economic policy and planning. This was at the cost, however, of disregarding the implications of a wider bargaining agenda for industrial relations law. These implications are now tackled in *People at Work*, which makes the theme of involvement along with fairness a basic starting-point for a new approach.

The statement recognises that, "there is no question of excluding the law from industrial relations. But it can be given a positive role — with new rights and protection for individual workers and their unions". The Tory approach is clearly "to shift the balance of power in society against working people". It has no strategy to reorganise industry except by strengthening employers' control over the key decisions which affect Britain's economic performance.

Authority

Consequently, *People at Work* notes that the Government's trade union legislation "encourages authoritarian management; it treats workers as isolated individuals and limits their freedom to combine and act together in pursuit of their interests; and it is designed to unleash the market forces of 'competition', ignoring the wider need for co-operation and involvement in the process of industrial change".

After seven years of this bracing 'free enterprise' climate, however, employers have failed to deliver the investment and growth required to maintain living standards and create employment in a post-North Sea oil economy. Labour's economic proposals, on the other hand, are designed to influence and co-ordinate the necessary investment decisions, but not just by substituting for employers' prerogatives the all-powerful state of traditional socialism.

Instead, recent TUC-Labour Party statements have placed the emphasis on greater workforce influence through extensions of industrial democracy. This is viewed as a more realistic and broadly-based method of changing enterprise behaviour. It also suggests a new vision of democratic socialism, in which working people themselves are able to shape their own future.

Accordingly, Labour's declared aim as the 'Party of production' will be realised not by the state attempting to direct the economy from the centre but rather acting as an 'enabling force' (Eatwell and Green, 1984).

Bargaining

Taking up the theme of democracy, the *People at Work* statement grounds it in both the experience and potential of collective bargaining. This is presented as "an effective counterweight to concentrations of power in Britain's economy. It thus has a vital democratic role in making decisions accountable to workers and society".

The statement accepts, as we have seen, that the law can assist bargaining and organisation, as well as restrict it. The old 'voluntarist' idea that the law has no place in industrial relations has long been superseded by events. The only relevant question for a Labour Government is how legislation can be framed to provide maximum support for workers and their unions. The answer may be found in the development of collective bargaining itself over the last two decades.

Trends at Work

Following the initial impetus given by productivity bargaining in the 1960s, a major shift has occurred in pay negotiations from national to plant and, increasingly, company level. This trend has continued in the 1970s and 80s, mainly in the private sector. It has given rise to an upsurge in shop steward activity and to 'joint union committees', which bring together different unions at the workplace to agree common negotiating positions.

Recent survey evidence shows that "multi-employer, industry-wide arrangements have continued to give way to single-employer bargaining at company or establishment level"; it also suggests that "the formal trappings of trade union organisation at the workplace have suffered little; recognition of unions, of senior stewards, and of closed shops was much the same as in the late 1970s" (Brown, 1986).

The shift in the level of bargaining has also been accompanied by a decentralisation of management, which has in turn led to the widespread growth of joint consultation arrangements. Although designed by employers for 'one-way' communication, these arrangements have often allowed union representatives to extend the *scope* of bargaining beyond wages into areas such as health and safety, training and new technology.

One major reason stems from the nature of industrial change itself: "New technology cannot be simply interpreted as a means by which management further extends its control over labour. In certain respects it can be claimed that management often exposes itself to a greater dependence on labour." (Batstone, 1985).

The latest studies indicate that the most successful examples of joint consultation "are firmly based on trade union organisation", (*Industrial Relations Review and Report*, July 1986). Consultation which does not serve as an adjunct to bargaining degenerates inevitably into triviality.

Planning

Workers' influence tends to be strongest in the large and medium-sized companies which dominate the economy. These are the very companies whose decisions will be crucial to the success of an interventionist industrial policy. Consequently, it makes sense for workforce representatives to participate not just in the decisions of their own company but also in setting external plans and priorities. This will be facilitated by a further, more recent trend in industry.

There is evidence of increasing interdependence between firms in key sectors of the economy as a result of greater specialisation in the product market. This makes the *sector* a strategic focus for planning in a way it could not become in the past. The sector committees of the National Economic Development Council (NEDC) are the obvious channel through which workers can contribute to the formulation of wider priorities and develop their own initiatives beyond the individual enterprise (Green and Wilson, 1983).

The NEDC's main concern is to get sector strategies translated into action at company level, but it is hampered by a lack of powers and resources. Even now, in a hostile environment, it is promoting links with joint bodies in the workplace. The sector committee for the paper and board industry, for example, is about to fund the training of shop stewards involved in workplace consultation bodies (*Financial Times*, 12th June, 1986).

Public Sector

Pay bargaining in the public sector is more centralised than in private manufacturing industry. Nevertheless, the potential for widening industrial democracy exists here too at every level of decision-making. Joint consultation machinery has — at least formally — been more highly developed in the public sector, but the agenda is similarly limited by the employer.

The public sector has also been turned into an industrial battleground in recent years, as the Government attempts to undermine pay bargaining and short-circuit existing consultation procedures. The *People at Work* statement argues that "the time is ripe to consider how the chief officers and senior board members of public industries are appointed".

Further, "in both the public industries and the public services, there is scope for imaginative experiments in industrial democracy". The degree to which the Party and TUC have digested the lessons of the public sector experiments of the 1970s is demonstrated by the more flexible approach to legislation in this area, as we see below.

Incomes Policy

The development of industrial democracy would not just overcome weaknesses in previous attempts at planning in Britain, but it could also supersede the traditional reliance on incomes policy. Although this issue can become complicated, the experience of imposing norms or maximum limits on pay is all too clear — they simply have not worked for any length of time.

The resources released by pay restraint have always tended to go into profits rather than investment, defeating the purpose of a wider industrial strategy. And the eventual collapse of restraint due to bargaining pressures and anomalies has inevitably given rise to a wages explosion, defeating the purpose of the incomes policy — and bringing about the collapse of the government which introduced it.

The traditional alternative to incomes policy is deflation, which the Tories have imposed with unprecedented intensity. Their industrial relations legislation is partly designed to reinforce competition in the labour market by removing the 'rigidities' which prevent it from operating in the way demanded by their economic theory ('Market Principles and Union Power', *Tribune*, 22 February, 1985). This approach has not worked either.

A New Approach

So the Government has now called for 'profit-sharing' as a further means of securing pay restraint. The Chancellor wants to move to a system where "a significant proportion of an employee's remuneration depends directly on the company's profitability". There is also an increasing emphasis on individual employee share ownership to create the illusion of involvement.

If all these approaches are an attempt to substitute for industrial democracy, perhaps it is time to try the real thing! Increased control by workers over investment decisions through extensions of collective bargaining will allow a proper balance between investment and consumption to be struck within the bargaining process itself, thus making external pay norms superfluous and unnecessary.

A previous TUC-Labour Party statement, *Partners in Rebuilding Britain* (1983), put it like this:

"Workers will have greater influence over these key aspects of company planning — including the allocation of resources between investment and consumption — as they exercise their new statutory rights through joint union committees and contribute to strategies for their industries in sector planning committees. This means that they will assume a new responsibility for the planning of real incomes as an aspect of the production process."

The significance of industrial democracy in the context of pay bargaining is also recognised in the statement on *Low Pay*, which points to the need for "a forum for relating all aspects of company performance including (the) allocation of profits..." This approach would be supplemented by a 'fair wages' strategy to ensure a proper 'rate for the job' and, in particular, comparability in the non-profit public sector.

Legislation

A major theme of *People at Work* is that new legal rights will be required for workers to "promote a radical extension of industrial democracy". These rights should be designed to support tendencies inherent in the development of voluntary collective bargaining ('A Positive Industrial Relations Framework', Prescott, 1985).

As the statement itself makes clear, the approach is "not to impose any particular model or method of industrial democracy", but "to widen the collective bargaining agenda beyond wages to crucial investment decisions — decisions which determine the performance of companies and the economy as a whole". The new rights would act as a 'catalyst' for the extension of democratic involvement and accountability, "not only within the enterprise but also beyond it, in sector and national planning".

Although the precise nature of the proposed planning system is not set out, the statement reaffirms Labour's commitment to industrial democracy as the basis of any new system. This will take the form of rights to information, consultation and representation at the workplace.

Information and Consultation

As a first step, employees and their representatives need information about the plans and activities of the enterprise if they are to play a constructive role. A general right to disclosure of information "would expand the range of issues covered and make the company's books available for inspection". A right to information will only be effective, however, if it is located in the context of a right to be consulted *before* decisions are taken that may be harmful to workers' interests.

A right of continuous consultation "would put union representatives in a stronger position to make use of information". It could be operated by representatives of workers and management in a permanent joint consultation committee, modelled on the existing safety committees. This would become a 'planning committee', as proposed in previous TUC-Labour Party statements, and would provide a key link with the wider planning system.

Modest information and consultation rights have already been put forward for consideration in a recent European Community draft directive — the 'Vredeling' directive. This would give employee representatives access to management in the national subsidiaries of large companies and multinationals, and to their world-wide headquarters.

As *People at Work* points out, the directive "would help to strengthen international trade union links". So it was hardly surprising when, after a vigorous campaign by employers' organisations and multinational companies themselves, the UK Government blocked the directive in the European Council of Ministers.

Representation

A planning committee would boost workers' influence in economic management, but without involving responsibility for the whole enterprise. A corresponding disadvantage is that it would lack the power which would flow from being part of the administrative structure. To argue that workers should not become involved at all in the process of management and administration is to perpetuate not their independence but their subordination to the employer.

As a further step in new legislation, the *People at Work* statement therefore proposes a new right for employees to be represented "up to, and including, boards of management". This right would allow them to develop "a permanent and continuous influence over all aspects of enterprise planning". While it is similar in form to the 1976 Bullock Committee recommendations, it starts from a different angle.

The Bullock proposals became largely identified with a 'company law' approach to industrial democracy. A criticism made by trade unionists was that worker directors would be superimposed on collective bargaining. This time, Labour's approach will allow employees and their representatives to use a *series* of new rights to promote the natural extension of bargaining.

According to *People at Work*, these rights would be exercised through the "recognised unions" in a company or establishment, although the precise arrangement would have to take account of "the diversity of industrial relations structures in Britain today".

Certainly, "new methods of joint union working and co-operation" will be necessary to formulate a coherent bargaining position in relation to employers. The development of joint union committees, as we have seen, already goes some way in this direction, but the problems faced by workers in the present environment should not be underestimated.

Support for Rights

The exercise of new rights will lead to an increase in workplace employee and union activity. This will require an extension of legal protection and more resources from employers so that workers can become effectively involved in the organisation of the enterprise.

'People at Work' calls for the "provision of adequate time and workplace facilities by employers" in the context of 'membership participation in unions', as well as bargaining with employers. This would apply also to the development of industrial democracy. Indeed, past experience seems to show that expanding control by workers over the job is the most effective way of strengthening their influence inside their own organisations.

The concept of 'appropriate time' during which employees are entitled to hold meetings will need to be extended, as will the range of protected activities. Rights to time-off should cover meetings at the workplace and outside conferences. Labour's planning and workers' rights legislation will thus provide for new facilities and resources, including "access to education", so that workers can play a full part in Britain's recovery.

Strikes

What happens if workers need to put economic pressure on their employer through industrial action? This brings us back to the issue raised at the beginning. As *People at Work* points out, "providing workers with an opportunity to influence and participate in company decisions will assist in avoiding disputes. Yet the right to strike is fundamental for workers and their unions".

The limiting notion of 'trade dispute', which invited judicial intervention in the 1970s, is therefore dropped in favour of a positive right to strike combined with a modified immunity, which underpins Labour's new industrial democracy rights. This 'twin-track' approach now reads as follows:

— "It will be lawful for workers to organise or take part in a strike or other industrial action in defence of their interests. The range of issues on which workers could properly seek to influence an employer would need to reflect the wider collective bargaining agenda envisaged in our proposals on industrial democracy."

— "Unions organising a withdrawal of labour or other form of industrial action will have comprehensive legal protection against actions in tort, contract and equity."

This approach means that for the first time workforces will be able to bring direct pressure to bear over the key investment decisions relating to expansion and closures, product development, mergers and takeovers, plant and office location and all aspects of technological change (Ewing, 1986; Wilson, 1986).

Limits

The possibility of *some* limitation on the right to strike is implied in the proposal for a new tribunal or labour court to consider "the validity of industrial action". While the way in which injunctions are granted against unions is to be "substantially modified", only *ex parte* injunctions (the kind which employers can order over the telephone) are to be prohibited. The nature of the tribunal is not spelt out in the statement, so further discussion will no doubt have to follow.

It is firmly maintained, however, that the provision for secret ballots on strikes and uinion executive elections "would in no way give employers, or their customers or suppliers, any opportunity to seek injunctions and damages against a union". In contrast with the 1984 Trade Union Act, this right is confined to union members only.

The statement rejects "the often-made charge that unions are undemocratic bodies". It supports membership involvement with rights to time-off and workplace facilities. In a speech to this year's SOGAT conference, Neil Kinnock argued that ballots must have "practical effects as well as results" (*Financial Times*, 12th June, 1986). They cannot just be ignored by employers. It follows that they should entitle workers to positive new rights.

For example, where a ballot goes in favour of industrial action, there is a case for providing employees with a right to social security payments, and making dismissal automatically unfair. The best way to encourage ballots is to show that they can bring tangible benefits to those who participate in them.

This may not be an ideal position from the viewpoint of union responses to the TUC consultation, which generally favoured the complete removal of statutory balloting requirements. Nevertheless, it does accurately reflect the compromise reached in TUC-Labour Party discussions. It is not our purpose here to look in any detail at the precise form of this compromise, which may depend on further discussions at the TUC and Party conferences. Some possible options have been set out by shadow employment spokesman, John Prescott ('Labour to curtail power of courts', *Financial Times*, 6th June, 1986).

Partnership

Some say that the new *People at Work* statement is a return to *In Place of Strife*. Others say it amounts to a 'charter for trade union power'. Still others argue that, at least on the balloting issue, "the document has emerged in so verbose and garbled a form that it is difficult for any voter to make out Labour's policy" (*Economist*, 26th July, 1986).

Can all these observations be true at once? If so, there is clearly more work to be done. If not, the reader will judge which description, if any, fits the bill.

An important question that does need to be resolved is the *timescale* for repeal and replacement legislation. The TUC is committed by last year's Congress to seeking repeal "during the first parliamentary session of a Labour Government" (Composite Motion No.2). Assuming repeal and replacement are to be simultaneous, Labour must be ready with a draft Workers' Rights Bill on coming to office, so that unnecessary delay can be avoided.

The key issues of new legislation in the statement are clear: "Our commitment to industrial democracy, fair wages and job security offers a solid foundation for the new partnership we propose between the next Labour government and people at work". This chapter has shown how the proposals for industrial democracy will contribute to Labour's partnership and, after the next election, to a new kind of economic planning and socialism in Britain.

References

Batstone, E. (1985), *Union Structure and Strategy in the Face of Technical Change*, Blackwell.

Brown, W. (1986), "The Changing Role of Trade Unions", *British Journal of Industrial Relations*, XXIV/2.

Eatwell, J. and Green, R. (1984), "Economic Theory and Political Power", in Pimlott, B. (ed), *Fabian Essays in Socialist Thought*, Heinemann.

Ewing, K.D. (1986), "The Right to Strike", *Industrial Law Journal*, forthcoming.

Green, R. and Wilson, A., (1983), "The Future Course of Planning", in Topham, T. (ed), *Planning the Planners*, Spokesman.

Hepple, B., (1986), "Restructuring Employment Rights", *Industrial Law Journal*, 15/2.

Labour Party (1984), "Workers Rights in Europe", NEC Statement.

McCarthy, W. (1985) *Freedom at Work*, Fabian Tract, No. 508.

Prescott, J., (1985), "Planning for Full Employment", Parliamentary Spokesman's working group.

TUC (1986), "Industrial Relations Legislation', Consultative Document.

TUC — Labour Party (1982), "Economic Planning and Industrial Democracy", Joint Statement.

— (1983), "Partners in Rebuilding Britain', Joint Statement.

— (1985), "A New Partnership: A New Britain", Joint Statement.

— (1986), "People at Work: New Rights, New Responsibilities", Joint Statement.

— (1986), "Low Pay: Policies and Priorities", Joint Statement.

Wilson, A., (1986), "The Future of Labour Law: 'Positive Rights' and 'Immunities'", *The Industrial Tutor*.

Chapter 4

Trade Unionism, Public Policy and the Law

Bob Fryer

The Dilemmas

We are now within two years of a General Election. The coming months will be critical for both British trade unions and the Labour Party in the development of policies to set before the electorate and to campaign for at the General Election. It is already evident that, within the Labour Party at least, some leaders regard the related issues of rights at work, trade unionism and collective bargaining as decidedly uncongenial terrain for a successful electoral campaign.

The potential problems are easy to predict, although less easy to resolve. First, and perhaps most threatening for the Labour Party, is the risk that the Conservative Party (and indeed the Alliance) will be swift to pounce upon any proposals that they feel able to portray as a retreat from the strategy of 'reforming' industrial relations and trade unionism that Mrs Thatcher's Government has made one of its principal and most successful political platforms. Hostile commentators in political circles and the media (and even in some trade union quarters) will also be eager to criticize what they will characterise as a restoration or extension of so-called 'union privileges'. This certain pitfall alone is likely to cause hesitation in Labour (and some union) ranks in giving political priority to a programme of industrial relations and trade union initiatives in the coming period.

A second, related problem is the immense difficulty of achieving a genuine consensus within the trade union movement about what is now desirable. The difficulties here could be many-sided. In addition to some of the well-known (and occasionally exaggerated) political differences between unions, there are also likely to be equally sharp differences of emphasis *within* unions, as different levels of organisation give priority to their own most pressing causes. Equally important, it must be recognised that different unions and different groups of workers face quite different employment circumstances and difficulties and, irrespective of their broader political preferences, they will each wish to secure policies adequate to deal successfully with their own immediate problems. Quite obviously, bitter divisions amongst and within trade unions in the run-up to an election could be quite disastrous for both the Labour Party and the unions. On the other hand, an imposed consensus and a failure now to thrash out genuine differences of opinion could simply store up problems for the future so that, in the event of a Labour Government being elected, bitter and destructive conflicts could break out during its life with disastrous consequences.

The drift of the argument so far might well incline the prudent to steer well clear of the whole business of trade unionism and rights at work. Perhaps needless to say, such a course of action is neither desirable nor possible. From the point of view of millions of British workers as well as the unions, something urgently needs to be done to stop the erosion of their protections at work and the decline in union membership and influence. In any case, the TUC is committed to a review of industrial relations legislation and has already produced its own 'consultative document' which provided the focus for debate at its March 1986 Special Congress.[1] Similarly, the TUC General Council and its Employment Policy and Organisation Committee have been giving urgent consideration to draft proposals, especially those emanating from the TUC-Labour Party Liaison Committee. A joint statement *People at Work: New Rights, New Responsibilities* has been agreed in time to go to the autumn conferences of both the TUC and Labour Party.[2] In the midst of this discussion, certain trade union leaders, some politicians, academic specialists, journalists and union-watchers are also coming forward with their own ideas and proposals.[3] With all of this activity afoot, there is very little chance that the undoubtedly tricky issues can be easily pushed aside. In any case, critics of the Labour Party and the TUC, including especially the Prime Minister and her Conservative ministerial colleagues, will be only too delighted to open up the wounds if they suspect that the unions and Labour Party are simply being coy or are even dissimulating about the matter. Not, of course, that all the likely critics are outside the labour movement. There will be some equally eagle-eyed sceptics from within who will be determined to spot and denounce retreats, climb-downs, humbug, compromises, sell-outs and dilutions of the socialist project!

In the circumstances, it might be tempting for the TUC, constituent unions and the Labour Party to say as little as possible about industrial relations and trade union policies. Recognising that *something* must be said, some cautious advisers will counsel against an attempt to dot too many "i's" and cross too many "t's". There is a lot of merit in such an approach. First, it avoids excessively early commitment and its related risk, rigidity. Secondly, it provides scope for further essential consultation and elaboration. Thirdly, it acknowledges the necessarily emergent and developing character of employment relations in which 'step by step' approaches are valuable. Fourthly, it allows for a strategy for industrial relations to be linked into other proposed Labour policies. Fifthly, and perhaps most importantly, it provides some room for manoeuvre for both the Labour Party and the TUC once (if) Labour gets elected to government to take stock of the situation it is then confronted with.

Despite all of these advantages of what might be called a 'minimalist' or 'detail-less' approach, even this is not without its problems. After all, it is difficult to organise a successful campaign around a programme that has given too little attention to practical implications (as was discovered with the Alternative Economic Strategy or AES in 1983). Again, if critics and opponents start digging deep into the possible implications of a general policy, different answers might well be given by different respondents (as also happened in the past with, for example, Labour defence strategy). But, perhaps most important of all, there are some trade unionists and active Labour supporters who fear that a 'minimalist' or 'detail-less' perspective at this stage will leave things too open and give far too much freedom of room to manoeuvre to a Labour Party and leadership which, once elected to government office, might fail to deliver what they regard as essential. The reasons could be manifold and certainly need not merely imply bad faith or treachery, but could easily include inner-party dissent, the balance of political forces in the House of Commons, intransigence from the House of Lords, progressive undermining by the judges and courts, hostility from the City and business, unabated press campaigns and massive pressure from international capital, the European Economic Community (EEC) and other international political and financial allies, including the United States. If such scenarios are acknowledged to be possible, then opponents of the 'minimalist' approach will argue for firmer and more detailed commitments which will line up trade union and working class support in readiness for potential mobilisation to help a new Labour government carry through its project. Indeed, they will go further and point out that such an approach to politics is both essential for socialist advance and necessary in the circumstances of class conflict prevailing in Britain.

What all of this adds up to is that, whilst it is now both necessary and unavoidable for trade unions and the Labour Party to propose positive policies for trade unionism and for people at work, those proposals must be based upon the fullest possible debate and consultation with the unions and Party. Neither group should attempt to 'bounce' the other or to rush headlong into policies until the implications of its approach have been carefully thought through. In particular, supposed electoral advantage should be eschewed where it seems likely that such a short-term tactic will only store up serious trouble for the future. In all of this, care should also be taken to ensure that trade union and Labour Party members are not treated as merely passive by-standers. Their consent will need to be won not simply for the ideas being proposed but also for their practical implementation. That will require active support, right from initial discussions through to applications in practice. Such involvement would not only facilitate the establishment of a fully debated and genuinely agreed position (thereby reducing the risk of conflicting interpretation to critics) but would also provide a firm platform for a wider campaign in the trade union and labour movements and amongst the electorate generally.

Setting the Context
Bearing in mind the points made in the previous section about the immediate, pre-General Election consideration of any proposals for trade unionism, collective bargaining and rights at work, it is essential also to set out the broader political, economic and legal context in which proposals must be judged. The key features of that context are set out in the second section of this chapter.

Employment structure
Perhaps the most important and striking characteristic of the present context of any proposals is the remarkable shift that has recently taken place in the structure and composition of the British labour force. Over the past 20 years, but particularly over the last decade, the British labour force has manifested profound changes. Not only has there been a dramatic shift from extractive and manufacturing industries to service employment, but this has been accompanied by a growth in public sector (especially public service) work, in women's paid employment, in so-called white collar work, in part-time jobs and in temporary

employment.[4] In the circumstances of a long-term secular upward drift of unemployment (sharply increased since 1979) and massive industrial restructuring and factory closures, young workers are entering paid employment relatively later and older workers are retiring from work earlier, each largely because of the sheer absence of job opportunities.[5] Within these overall changes, employer strategies have also shifted. Although much fashionable attention is given to the introduction of new technologies, of equal importance have been changes in work organisation and labour processes, the reassertion of managerial authority and prerogatives, a drive towards increased efficiency and productivity, greater reliance upon flexible, part-time, casual and other so-called 'peripheral' workers, deskilling of work and a sharp decline in the use of training and qualification in industry.[6] It is not possible to do more than sketch out these changes here, but it is evident that any policy for rights at work and trade union organisation must needs address itself to these fundamental changes and to the workers most affected by them. They include not only the young job-less and the older long-term unemployed, but also women workers, part-time employees, migrant workers and their offspring, workers in older, declining centres of industry and housing and those in hitherto unprotected and badly organised sectors of the economy.

Union image

A second, key feature of the context of present proposals for reform concerns the standing of trade unionism and trade union organisation, especially the popular 'image' of trade unionism. Despite the interlude of the Social Contract (and contrary to popular opinion about its so-called 'pro-union' character), it is possible to trace a growing climate of anti-unionism and public hostility to trade unionism in Britain over the past 30 years or so. A convenient starting point might be the Conservative Inns of Court publication *A Giant's Strength*, in 1958, which declared that even those who sympathetically accept the need for "powerful spokesmen to represent the needs of the working man (sic)...are now apprehensive that the great powers the unions have been given may be used tyrannically or in a manner contrary to the best interests of the country as a whole."[7]

Throughout the 1960s, under both Conservative and Labour Governments, attacks were made upon trade unionism, especially over alleged restrictive practices, excessive unofficial industrial conflict and so-called 'wage-push' inflation. The *Report* of the Donovan Commission did little to deflect these challenges and both *In Place of Strife* and the Conservative Government's

1971 Industrial Relations Act fuelled attacks on trade unionism by the mass media, politicians, employers and even some trade union members themselves. Ironically, allegations of privileged status for unions, cosseted workers and cosy deals between the trade unions and Labour leadership only added to the poor public image of the unions in the social contract years of 1975-78. In any case, that relationship was soon to break down in the bitter accusations and counter-accusations about cuts in public expenditure, wage controls and recriminations about the conflagration of the 1978-79 'winter of discontent'. Mrs Thatcher's Conservative Government soared to power in 1979 on a surge of anti-unionism and opposition to collective organisation. This was turned to devastating effect not only in the successive 'step-by-step' legislation of 1980, 1982 and 1984 but also in her wider (un)employment strategy, her campaign for the 'deregulation' of business and enterprise, her powerful advocacy of privatisation and the widespread reduction of workers' employment and wage protection policies and arrangements initiated by the Conservatives from 1979 onwards.

Mention is made of this crescendo of public hostility to trade unionism and workers' collective organisation not in order to accord legitimacy to such opposition, nor yet to imply that it requires a timid and hesitant response. But its successes should not be underestimated and the practical effects, including the widespread preference for *individual* as against *collective* methods of decision-making in unions and the popularity of union-bashing, need to be countered. Such a counter attack cannot proceed on the basis of an alternative legislative framework alone, nor can it be expected to develop out of an excessively cautious or minimalist approach. However, if trade unionism and support for trade unionism are to be rebuilt and extended to include new groups of workers, it is evident that a positive strategy of some sort must be mapped out. In all likelihood, such a strategy would have to be given a wider brief than just traditional 'industrial relations'. It would also need to extend beyond the important expansion of individual rights at work if trade unionism, collective bargaining and the broader issue of democracy at work are all to be the beneficiaries of such a strategy and the dangers of unofficialism and inter-union conflicts are to be avoided.

Legal intervention

A third, and critical, element of the present context is, of course, the law. Too often this feature of the present attack upon workers' rights and trade unionism is accorded sole priority and this is plainly erroneous. Except in an indirect way, the vast majority of workers and trade unionists have not been touched by the so-called 'anti-union' Employment Acts of 1980 and 1982, and their major interest in the 1984 Trade Union Act resulted in the overwhelmingly successful political fund ballot campaign. However, such an evaluation of the impact of law upon workers is over-simplified for four reasons.

First, it seriously underestimates the *indirect* effect of Conservative legislation upon workers, trade unionism, collective bargaining and, not least, employers. There can be no doubt that the Tory framework of law has greatly contributed towards the weakening of trade union organisation and the scope for solidarity action, has vastly increased the chances of legal intervention in union affairs and collective bargaining, has imposed rule-changes upon unions, has cost the unions a small fortune in campaign and administrative costs and has buttressed managerial resolve. Secondly, the law has intervened in industrial disputes not only in the form of the 1980, 1982 and 1984 legislation, but also in the increased use of the common law and criminal law against workers and their organisations. This was seen to most dramatic effect, of course, during the miners' strike where the 'specialised' industrial relations legal framework was virtually insignificant by comparison with other legal attacks and devices including public order offences, highway offences and the remarkable imposition of receivership on the National Union of Mineworkers (NUM).[8] Similarly, changes in the legal regulation of social security benefits were also used against striking miners as they have been against other workers in dispute and their families. Thirdly, although the three main Acts have provided a major thrust for the Conservative Government against the unions, of equal importance have been reductions in various forms of employment protection, including increasing the qualifying periods in employment and hours spent at work, abolishing minimum wage provisions and reducing the jurisdiction and powers of Wages Councils. Fourthly, even before the Conservative Government's election in 1979 there was already growing evidence of the so-called 'juridification' of industrial relations, in which some judges demonstrated that they had lost none of their originality and partiality in introducing new restrictions upon workers' actions, despite the (supposedly advantageous) legislative framework established under the (amended) Trade Union and Labour Relations Act and Employment Protection Act, introduced by the Labour Government of 1974-1979.[9] On the other hand, of course, it does not follow that all legislative incursions into the employment relation are necessarily undesirable or at least unavoidable given the present balances of forces in industry. Roy Lewis, for one, has argued that "juridification need not have a pejorative taint. It should be distinguished from unnecessary legalism...it is likely and, in some instances desirable, that employers and unions will be increasingly influenced by legal norms and procedures."[10]

Although it is notoriously dangerous to generalise, the lessons of the past for trade unions, including the recent past under Labour-promoted as well as Tory-inspired laws, strongly suggest that, where the law and its institutions are not directly hostile to workers and their organisations, they are at best uncomfortable and perfidious supporters. It seems that not only do the legal turn of mind and the natural sympathies of the court and judiciary provide a most unpromising basis for expanding workers' and trade unions' rights at work, but also that juridical and legal presuppositions about power and organisation in employment are severely at odds with political and economic reality. In these circumstances, it would be a very great mistake for Labour or the TUC to place a framework of law at the centre of its new strategy. It would be equally foolish and naive not to anticipate some of the potential interventions of the courts, even where no supposedly positive role was provided for them, especially given the importance of the common law, judicial review and the superior role of the Court of Appeal and House of Lords in the British legal system. Similarly, it would be erroneous to make workers' rights, for example, in respect of picketing or public demonstration in pursuance of a dispute, dependent on the support or discretion of a police force which has recently shown itself to be deeply antagonistic to the aims and methods of trade unions. Moreover, were police actions to be challenged in the courts by unions, the police might reasonably expect judgement in their favour on the strong grounds that their public responsibilities extend much further than the relatively narrow terrain of work and employment.

Trade union organisation
A fourth major feature of the present context concerns the level and extent of trade union organisation. On paper at least, trade union organisation in Britain reached an all-time high in 1979, the year the present Conservative Government first came to power. According to statistics published by the Certification Officer, total trade union membership in 1979 was 13,250,000 or about 55 per cent of the employed labour force.[11] Not only had trade unions never before counted so many members amongst their number,

but such a density of organisation was also unprecedented. Between 1974 and 1979 total union membership had increased by 1,500,000 or 13 per cent, despite the fact that the number of unions had fallen by more than 10 per cent.

Of course, it is important to remember that these increases in numbers and percentage of workers organised had taken place against the background, already described, of changes in the structure of employment and the beginnings of an upward trend in unemployment. At the same time, sceptical commentators have pointed out that *some* of this new trade unionism was stronger on paper than in reality and depended heavily upon the increased provision of facilities to trade unions at work, especially the availability of deductions of trade union subscriptions at source (the 'check off'). Such facilities were of particular importance in the public services, where unions such as NUPE, NALGO, SCPS, CPSA and COHSE made great strides. Doubters feared that, in a downturn and in circumstances less favourable to trade unionism, some of this trade unionism would be exposed as resting on weak organisation and low levels of membership commitment. Some evidence of the validity of this suspicion is given by the statistics after 1979 when levels or density of trade unionism (including in the public services) actually fell at a faster rate than levels of employment. By 1984, total trade union membership just exceeded 11,000,000 workers or 47 per cent (a fall of 2,250,000 or 16.6 per cent in just five years) with some trade unions, such as the giant TGWU, manifesting dramatic membership losses.

In taking proper account of this decline in trade union membership, care must be taken not to exaggerate the scale of the setbacks suffered by the trade unions and collective bargaining. Despite the development of anti-union and union-busting tactics by some employers[12], it would be wrong to assume that trade unionism is being rolled back on all fronts. Eric Batstone, reporting on one detailed enquiry undertaken in manufacturing industry in 1983, cautioned against hasty assumptions that a massive and widespread reverse has occurred since 1979 in collective bargaining, trade union organisation and shop floor power:

> "The range of bargaining is still significant...(and) formal agreements similarly cover a fairly wide range of issues, but do not appear to be associated either with lower levels of negotiation or with reduced steward influence."[13]

And this was despite some setbacks at the hands of a minority of 'macho' managements over the previous five years.

Even so, it is widely acknowledged that where there has been some recent limited growth in employment, this has not taken place in traditionally well-organised sectors but in self-employment, part-time, seasonal and temporary work, home work and private services. It is in such sectors of the economy, as John Edmonds has observed, that workers'

> "...real concern is getting off first base: winning the right to trade union membership, raising poverty wages, avoiding discrimination or victimisation, dealing with arbitrary and aggressive management."[14]

A new strategyfor trade union organisation needs urgently to be oriented towards the situation of these workers as well as to the wider problem of a relative and all too sharp decline in the level and density of trade union membership overall in the nineteen-eighties.

The unacceptable face

A fifth, and final aspect of the present context also deserves comment, however brief. This is the pitiable and quite unacceptable plight of British workers treated like pawns in some global game of economic and political chess as employers, government, departments of state and rivals on the stockmarket have fought amongst themselves to determine the future of several British companies and hence of their workforces. Farce has combined closely with gross irresponsibility as the relative powerlessness of British workers was starkly revealed in the dramas surrounding Westland Helicopters and the abortive sell-off of parts of British Leyland. Of particular piquancy was the manipulation on television of helicopter workers in a social club during the so-called 'Westland affair', where they were allowed to voice their support for the favoured 'American option' of a take-over by Sikorsky. One wonders what expression of workers' opinions would have been canvassed in even this insultingly superficial way had their views supported alternative (especially radical!) options. Similarly, miners, steelworkers and shipbuilders have been both by-standers to and victims of political and managerial decision-making over which they could exercise very little direct and constructive influence. By and large the workers were either kept in the dark until the last minute or were bullied and seduced into accepting closure and contraction by a combination of unrelenting propaganda and the bait of redundancy payments.

Against all of this, it has to be remembered how recent was the unenthusiastic reception given by the British trade unions to the so-called 'Bullock' proposals for extending industrial democracy and how little progress was made on planning agreements and workers' plans. Moreover, research on the public sector experiments in industrial democracy in the British Steel Corporation and the Post Office has also suggested a very limited and largely ineffectual role for workers and trade union representatives on the Board.[15] Not that this simply means that the only strategy left for workers at the point of production or in the offices, schools and canteens is a stand-off on the whole issue of participation and control. As Cressey and MacInnes have argued,

"The fact that it is the employers' side which often makes the running on 'industrial democracy' suggests at once the weakness and the strength of capital."[16]

What is required, argue the authors, are analyses and practices "...with the aim of exploring the potential for prefigurative forms within capitalism that point beyond it rather than patch it up."[17]

Nobody can expect that search to be easy or rapidly successful, but it is already evident that experiments in co-operative self-management and in some local authority-funded initiatives are at least deserving of careful evaluation. The issue becomes ever more urgent as the organisation and structure of employment in Britain takes on an increasingly international and global dimension in which workers and whole communities and their interests depend critically upon decisions made in boardrooms and stockmarkets far beyond their ken or control.[18]

The Aims of a New Policy

Strengthening collective organisation

By now it should be obvious that a clear and vigorous policy is necessary not only to combat the changes and attacks outlined in the previous section but also to avoid the problems discussed initially. What is needed is a framework of policies which command widespread support based on understanding throughout the trade union movement and amongst working people generally. In this third section of the chapter a number of suggested aims and objectives of such a new policy are put forward for discussion. No doubt they will be amended and added to in the course of debate.

The fundamental aim in the coming period has been very clearly set out by the TUC in its own thorough review of its services and strategy and of the developing role of affiliated unions. After acknowledging the potential damage to trade unionism inherent in the current combination of recession, government hostility and social and economic restructuring, the TUC declares that

"The Movement therefore has to counter-attack to make known and understood the positive contributions unions make to British society. But getting the message across will not be enough. Unions must also prove their fitness to play a continuing role in the future. What is more, unions must be ready to change in order to continue to advance the interests of working people and their families."[19]

Such an approach places trade unionism and collective organisation at the centre of the stage. The aim is not to make the unions indirect and almost *sub rosa* beneficiaries of a clutch of new policies and protections aimed principally at individuals. On the contrary, the fundamental aim is to reshape and reorient a reformed trade unionism in such a way as to make it better able to serve the interests of existing members as well as to prove attractive and available to that half of the working population who are currently unprotected by trade union organisation.

Individual rights

This is not an argument implying that individual rights are unimportant or can simply be assumed to be properly taken care of in unions' collective organisation. Nor yet is it a denial of the contribution that extended individual rights might make to the expansion of trade union membership and influence. All of these matters need their full recognition and a convincing commitment from the trade union movement to embrace them as part of a genuine programme of reform. But, even so, and this must be emphasised, the argument has to be put the right way round and no amount of attention to matters of 'presentation' or 'public relations' should be allowed to reverse it. The simple fact is that merely to extend (potential) individual rights at work within the protection of tribunals, courts or committees *without* the parallel strengthening of trade union organisation and activity, will be only to widen *formal* rights. There can be no guarantee that, in the face of hostile or persuasive employers or when taking account of the economic constraints facing them as workers, individual employees will be able to avail themselves truly of those rights.

Similarly, it would be dangerous indeed to assume that the courts and judiciary will be properly vigilant in expanding workers' rights against the power of managements, companies and public employers when neither the remedies available to them nor their past record of preferring to enforce rights *against* unions gives any grounds whatsoever for such misplaced confidence. Individual rights and their dramatic improvement in work, inside trade unions and in the wider society are most important to extend citizenship, but in a society deeply characterised by vast inequalities of power, resources and financial security, it is naive and disingenuous to assume that such changes will be possible for individuals without a proportional extension of the collective strength of workers' organisations.

The role of law

In advancing the interests and strength of both individuals and their organisations at work and in the wider community, it is evident that law will have a part to play both in its 'regulatory' and 'auxiliary' forms, and more will be said about this later, but another aim of any new policies must be that they do not depend, make-or-break so to speak, upon the laws and the interpretations and limitations imposed upon them by the courts and the judiciary. If the aim is to widen both individual and collective influences over the processes and decisions which affect the lives of working people, then it would be foolhardy to expect to achieve such lofty and probably contested aims largely or even primarily upon a legal framework. Of course, social power to some extent is shaped and formed by legal relations, but not exclusively so and not without great difficulty. Judging by past experience, there can be little doubt that, with the possible exception of certain aspects of health and safety at work, collective bargaining rather than the law has provided the chief basis for the improvement of workers' terms and conditions of work, for the expansion of individual rights at work and for the widening of workers' influences over managerial control. This does not mean that collective bargaining to date has achieved all that it might nor yet that collective bargaining *alone* can constitute the source of greater industrial citizenship and popular control over employment and economic matters generally. But collective bargaining is a sound and tested pillar of such future developments and, more vigorously supported through public policy and reformed and revitalised from within through democratic change, its future contribution could represent a major element in a political programme for empowering people at work and in extending democracy in employment.

Widening appeal and organisation

If all of this is to carry conviction, it has to appeal not only to union leaders, union 'die-hards' and rank and file activists, but also to those sections of the working class largely by-passed or even ignored by existing trade union organisation. This means that it will not at all be sufficient for young workers or women or black workers or unemployed people to figure almost as an afterthought in trade union policies and programmes. Their interests cannot simply be 'tacked on' to existing provisions or proposals, nor can they be assumed to be an homogenous group of 'others', for each has its own plurality of interests and needs. Hence another aim must be to bring each of these groups and their constituent sub-groups to the centre of the trade union and collective bargaining stage.

Workers in private services are one good example of those to whom the trade union movement needs to extend genuine opportunites for union membership, for democratic and interesting participation and for improving the conditions of their lives. To date the unions' record (for all sorts of reasons, some good and some bad) in generating strong organisation among such workers is poor: union density in private services in 1948 was 14.5 per cent; by 1979, the 'peak' year for union organisation in Britain, it had risen to just 16.7 per cent. In the same period, overall density had increased from 45.2 per cent to 55.4 per cent and dramatic increases in organisation had been registered by white collar workers, in the public sector and in manufacture.[21] Admittedly, the problems of organising in private services are enormous and the constraints imposed by employers, the structure of the industries, the composition of the workforce and the availability of union resources all hinder expansion in this area. But the aim should be clear and, maybe, targets need now to be established: the rapid extension of union organisation and protection to workers in private services, say, by an improvement in density of five per cent per annum over five years.

There can be no doubting the challenge that this will represent to the trade union movement. Indeed, one possible danger of an emphasis upon individual rights at work might be that in the limited circumstances where workers are able to avail themselves of them, they will regard trade unionism and all of its complex paraphernalia as redundant and alien. As the General Secretary of GMBATU has written

> "For the vast majority of workers on this new front line, trade unionism is distant, belongs to other types of workers and is increasingly pre-occupied with very inward and frankly incomprehensible wrangles."[22]

It is precisely to overcome such problems that the TUC launched its own strategy and consultative document just over two years ago. It would now be a tragedy if the important matters and questions raised with affiliates in that document were to be effectively swept aside in the current and understandable debate about the future role of law in industrial relations. To the millions of workers in poorly or unorganised sectors and to the millions without jobs, a debate about the relative virtues of an 'immunities' as against a 'rights' approach must appear not simply arcane but must have a decidedly hollow ring!

Equality in work and in society

But we can go still further in elaborating these aims. If trade unions are to take seriously the Herculean task of organisation sketched out here and in their own documents, and if the provision of additional rights is to *assist* them in these endeavours, then the whole controversial question of equality and inequality at work will need to be opened up. This is indeed a daunting task for it touches upon every aspect of working life and trade union activity and extends well beyond the workplace into the home and the community. The implications extend not only to the vital issues of low pay and poverty already under discussion by the TUC-Labour Party Liaison Committee, but also embrace collective bargaining strategy and wages structures, training and career opportunities, combating racist and sexist oppression, widening genuine opportunities for democratic participation in trade unions, linking up with initiatives and demands within the wider community and contributing to the transcendence of the existing unequal sexual division of labour at work, in the wider society and at home. Nobody expects all of these tasks to be tackled simultaneously and such radical social changes cannot be expected to be accomplished overnight. But the issues cannot be avoided. If workers' rights and citizenship are to be widened and if trade union influence is to be extended, all of these matters and others not even mentioned here need to find their way on to main agendas for trade union action. That is a challenge not for the law, nor even for the drafters of policy statements and documents, but for the partnership of the British trade union and labour movements, for politicians and trade unionists.

A united approach

If the ambitions and challenging aims set out here are to be embarked upon, it will be important to secure not only consent within the trade union movement but also unity amongst trade unions. For all its faults, the British trade union movement has always benefited from having only one centre of organisation and authority. In this context, suggestions that could lead to a 'dual' system of trade unionism in this country, including two tiers of 'registered' and 'unregistered' or even 'certificated' and 'uncertificated' organisations, could be potentially divisive and could even wreck the chances of agreed reform. Apart from having a nasty echo of the 1971 Industrial Relations Act about them, such suggestions also open the door for litigation and judicial intervention.[23]

Some Key Assumptions

If the arguments in the previous sections have any merit, by now we should be in a position to lay out the key assumptions of a strategy for the expansion of workers' rights, trade unionism and collective bargaining in employment. They can be set out easily in summary fashion.

(a) It should be assumed that the most promising way of advancing is to place as much distance as is possible between workers and the law *and* workers' organisations and the law. The expansion of each of their influences over the world of work must not be tied to either statutory provision, juridical interpretation or judicial intervention.

(b) As a main starting point there should be wholesale repeal of the 1980 and 1982 Employment Acts and the 1984 Trade Union Act. All seek to confine and restrict trade union methods and objectives and all together provide too many opportunities to the courts, employers and recalcitrant members to seek early and disabling redress against alleged union breaches of law.

(c) There needs to be a rapid restoration of and expansion of the limited protections reduced or abolished since the Conservative Government came to power. However, extending protection should not critically depend upon legal action but on a substantially strengthened trade union organisation bolstered by public policy and the strategic deployment of public funds, contracts and priorities.

(d) Before embarking on any new statutory requirements in respect of either trade unions or employers, careful thought should be given to any proposals to ensure, as far as is possible, that no new grounds are given to the judiciary to curtail the pursuit of public policy or to set in train dangerous divisions within the trade union movement. (For example, by the courts finding in favour of employers' avoidance of statutory duties or by some institution or person erecting divisions between 'registered' and 'unregistered' or 'certificated' and 'non-certificated' trade unions.)

(e) Energy, imagination and public support should be given to the promotion and extension of collective bargaining for all workers throughout the economy.

(f) The state, trade unions and employers should be committed to a reform of collective bargaining to tackle particularly the complex matter of inequality and discrimination, especially insofar as this contributes to the continued oppression of women and migrant workers, young people at work and those suffering from some physical or other disability.

(g) Trade unions need to engage in a thorough and continuing review of their own practices, policies and structures to improve vastly the opportunities and occasions for participative democracy and enjoyable involvement.

(h) Variation and diversity should be expected and welcomed as inherent in the expansion of collective and individual influences and freedoms at work. Such an approach should help to avoid the rigidities of a 'one best way' approach and allow different historical development and circumstances to shape the particular arrangements, always provided those arrangements did not obstruct or avoid the fundamental aims and objectives already outlined.

(i) Wherever possible and practicable, assistance and support should be given to the development of self-regulating and relatively autonomous arrangements amongst workers, within trade unions and within collective bargaining. Again, such arrangements should not be free to frustrate the fundamental aims and objectives of public policy. Nor should such system of self-regulation cut across any voluntarily or democratically agreed rules established by trade unions, the TUC or the institutions of collective bargaining. Of course and in turn, each of these rule-making bodies would themselves need to demonstrate their active promotion of public policy.

(j) Experimentation and innovation should be positively encouraged, especially where there are good *a priori* grounds for believing that innovative approaches will extend collective and individual influence at work and contribute to the advancement of public policy.

(k) Widespread use should be made of public enquiry, report and recommendation in developing and promoting public policy. Public authorities, including government ministers and departments, local authorities, public corporations, etc. should be empowered to take account of employers' and trade union practices and any reports on these in determining their own policies and priorities, including any financial decisions.

(l) The public sector should be required and be sufficiently resourced to act as a model employer in promoting public policy in respect of employment as well as in using contract-compliance and other monitoring devices in obtaining services or providing support to private employers and other groups.

(m) The elaboration of public policies in respect of trade unionism, rights at work and collective bargaining, should be designed to be consistent with the development of other policies both in the field of employment (for example in respect of eliminating low pay or extending training) and in other fields (including especially social security, education and equal opportunities).

(n) A combination of rights and especially expanded immunities should be deployed to achieve the main aims of public policy in employment. Great care should be exercised:
(i) to learn from past experience, including under the provisions of the 1974-79 Labour Government (not to do so would be to leave the field open to imaginative constraints imposed by the judiciary);
(ii) to avoid a collision between the rights of individuals and the rights of collective organisation (not to do so would risk unofficialism, break-aways and splinters and place severe restrictions upon trade unions as organisations).

(o) It has to be assumed that a programme of reform and development will take some time to implement and will require advance on several fronts, some of which are dealt with in the next section. Apart from the opposition to some of the ideas which might be anticipated and the need to win active and enthusiastic consent for the programme, it is essential to remember that it will be implemented against a background of (hopefully diminishing) Thatcherite policies, laws and achievements. These will include high levels and long durations of unemployment, declining and constrained public services, privatisation, increased poverty, and a strengthening of organisations and institutions traditionally hostile to the labour movement. Whatever else should be assumed, it would be very prudent to assume a difficult and deeply contested process of implementing social change.

Developing the Framework

Process important
Before providing some detailed suggestions for further discussion, it is worth beginning by applauding the start that has been given to this process both within the TUC and the Labour Party, as well as by those individuals who have outlined their own ideas for reform. Debate and exchange of views are essential to both the democracy and the efficacy of the labour movement and, although it could have been hoped that the topic had been broached earlier, it is vital now to extend that debate as far as possible throughout the membership of trade unions and amongst workers, their families and communities. This is not intended simply as a rhetorical flourish but in the belief that the very *process* of establishing a new framework will not only test out ideas and the support for them, but is in itself an ingredient of widening the influence which workers exercise over decisions which affect them.

TUC and Labour Party initiatives
With this in mind, there is much to be welcomed in the review the TUC has initiated of the law through its consultative document, special Congress and soliciting of affiliates' views. There is no need to rehearse all the arguments and criticisms again here except to echo the point that too sanguine a view should not be taken of *either* a simple 'back to pre-1979 immunities' approach or a 'rely on extending individual rights' strategy. Getting the correct mix of immunities and rights is clearly very necessary, but such a difficult task needs not only to review the real opportunities which each promises but also to understand where they both fit in with wider perspectives which this chapter has attempted to begin to sketch out.

Similarly, there is evidence of much good work and thinking in the TUC-Labour Party Liaison documents, even if so far they generally lack the kind of appeal and popularity which it is assumed they will require if they are to serve as rallying points for the trade union movement and for workers generally. There are also potential problems and weaknesses which need to be addressed.

Although there is probably something to be gained in both public relations and political terms by couching the joint proposals in terms of 'responsibilities' as well as of 'rights', great care needs to be exercised not to place workers in a position where they (or their representative organisations) are expected to exercise responsibility *without* power.

Jobs campaign

Probably the chief ingredient of workers' power, and one which will do more to enhance their rights at work both individually and collectively than any framework of 'positive' law, is simply having paid work to do and the opportunity to do it, preferably with a genuine choice of competing opportunities. In this sense, the central component of a new approach to workers' rights and democracy at work must be Labour's 'Jobs and Industry' strategy. Not, of course, for jobs at any price but for paid work which will provide the essential springboard for the ideas outlined in this paper as in several proposals from the trade unions, Labour Party, TUC and other supporting individuals.

The cornerstone

If this starting point can be agreed, then it appears that the next step is to place the extension of workers' influence over their own lives and communities at the centre of a new strategy. This means underlining and emphasising the key role that needs to be given to workers for greater democratic participation, increased involvement, additional and accessible information, widened and deepened collective bargaining, and extended opportunities for acting together with other workers in pursuit of their legitimate interests. In my view, this should be the cornerstone of a new approach (in many ways, it is a very old one, at least in theory). Questions of the role of law, choices of method, and the best means of providing public support, should all be judged in the light of these central and fundamental commitments.

Public support

Bearing in mind all the arguments and assumptions which have already been advanced in this paper, it is my view that the promotion of such a strategy would be best served not through the agency of statute (although this will have some part to play) but by the provision of vigorous public support for reformed collective bargaining, democratic trade union organisation and the rapid increase in workers' influence over decision-making in work. Much evidence from the history of the British trade union movement suggests that progress for workers depends on the complex interplay and mutually supportive relationship of workers' own organisation and efforts on the one hand and overtly supportive public policy on the other. Sometimes the lead is given by one side of this dialectic; sometimes by the other. From time to time, they may even come into conflict. The concluding paragraphs of this chapter make some proposals for building upon that understanding.

An Industrial Democracy Commission
It is suggested that support for the approach which has been outlined in this chapter could be provided by the establishment of a wholly new public body to be entitled the Industrial Democracy Commission (IDC). Staffed on both a national and regional basis with suitably qualified personnel whose own backgrounds and expertise commanded confidence amongst trade unions and workers, the tasks and responsibilities of the IDC would be as follows.

(a) Aims and responsibilities
(i) To promote and extend:
(A) collective bargaining amongst all workers;
(B) membersip of and participation in democratic trade unions by workers;
(C) the individual and collective influence of workers over decisions by managers, employers and others that affect their lives;

(ii) To seek to help and establish (A), (B) and (C) where these do not exist or where their existence is unduly restricted or confined.

(iii) To undertake enquiries of both a particular and general kind amongst workers, employers, trade unions, government departments and such other bodies as may to the IDC from time to time seem appropriate.

(iv) To publish reports and recommendations of both a particular and general kind.

(v) To make proposals to Government in respect of amendments to existing legislation or legal procedures (including any necessary repeals) or of any necessary new legislation touching upon (A), (B) and (C), including company law.

(vi) To recognise and monitor the important role of the public sector as a model employer in respect of (A), (B) and (C).

(vii) To give attention to the interests of the immediate and wider community in the pursuit of (A), (B) and (C).

(viii) To encourage the development by trade unions, employers and their respective organisations of suitable arrangements to promote (A), (B) and (C).

(ix) To review employer and employer association and trade union procedures for the promotion of (A), (B) and (C).

(x) To give publicity and information on good practice in industry in respect of (A), (B) and (C).

(xi) To draw up codes of conduct, in consultation with trade unions, employers and their organisations in respect of (A), (B) and (C).

(xii) To provide information to ministers, government departments, local authorities and public corporations in respect of trade unions, employers and their organisations in respect of (A), (B) and (C), so that these bodies (ministers, etc.) may take that information into account in determining questions of policy, funding and the provision or continuation of contracts, etc.

(xiii) To disperse public funds, upon the recommendation of the TUC where affiliated unions are concerned, in respect of (A), (B) and (C), including for education and training, for publicity and information, for involvement and participation and generally to support the promotion of (A), (B) and (C).

(xiv) To draw up appropriate procedures, rules and systems of administration to carry out (i) to (xiii).

(xv) To report regularly to an appropriate Minister and Parliament on the progress achieved with (i) to (xiv).

(b) Powers and authority
(i) The idea of the IDC would be to create an entirely new body with a combination of the kind of powers currently exercised by such bodies as the Law Commission, Monopolies and Mergers Commission and the Advisory, Conciliation, and Arbitration Service (ACAS). The chief power would be to require the provision of documents and evidence to the staff of the Commission. The only sanction and the only unlawful act in

respect of the IDC itself should concern refusal to co-operate with enquiries or attempts to frustrate it in the pursuit of its duties. The Commission itself should impose no sanctions, but severe sanctions should be available both to the courts and (especially) to ministers where a refusal to co-operate can be demonstrated. Strict time limits for compliance with requests to co-operate would need to be laid down and obstructive or time-wasting tactics alone should be reported on and ministers, government departments, local authorities and public corporations should be empowered to take account of any such reports or information in determining their own policies, including funding and contractual arrangements.

(ii) Employers, associated employers, companies, employer organisations, trade unions, associations of workers and other such bodies should each be required to produce their own annual reports in respect of their own pursuit of (A), (B) and (C) , and companies should be required to include the same in their Annual Reports and Accounts.

(c) Criteria and evaluation
The IDC should seek to develop its own criteria and systems of evaluation in respect of (A), (B) and (C), always bearing in mind the key assumption of the importance of promoting pluralism in form and self-regulation in practice.

(d) Membership and preparation
The Governing Council of the IDC should be independent of Government and should draw equally upon independent members, nominees of the TUC and employers. It might be objected that to give any employer's representative the power (albeit on a public body) to make enquiry into independent trade unions is a dangerous and unacceptable step. This is a powerful argument and should not be dismissed lightly. However, it is essential that the IDC should command widespread public support and ammunition should not be provided to employers to campaign (amongst workers and others) against the alleged "bias" or "unfairness" of the IDC's governing body. At the same time great care should also be taken in the appointment and renewal of appointment of commissioners, bearing in mind these serious objections. The record of commissioners themselves should indicate their support for the policies to be upheld and promoted by the IDC and their background and attitudes should command confidence. If necessary, a thorough education and

training programme should be developed for IDC commissioners and senior staff and only those successfully completing such courses should be appointed to or continue to hold office with the IDC. The IDC itself might also sponsor a series of courses of study for trade unions, employers and public servants in respect of the issues of democracy at work.

(e) Relationship to other initiatives
It should be clear that the IDC would represent only one of several initiatives aimed at widening democracy and participation, extending industrial citizenship and strengthening of workers' individual and collective rights at work. Other pertinent initiatives, which the IDC would need to keep under close review, would include the fields of education, consumer rights, local democracy, national and regional planning, and the development of production for social use. All of these promise an exciting and potentially popular programme and all would touch upon the proposed work of the IDC.

Ballots

One especially important and ticklish subject that the IDC would need to examine would be the whole area of ballots in trade unionism, collective bargaining, and before industrial action. The temptation here might be to rush ahead and declare policy or even legislate before careful thought has been given to the proper and varied role ballots might make in the world of work. Those urging immediate action would, probably, cite what they regard as widespread and growing public and union membership support for ballots, especially individual, secret ballots. No doubt, there is some strength in this assumption, but if its adherents are correct and, given that many unions have already amended their rules to include greater use of ballots, there is little danger of a rapid retreat from the use of ballots whilst a more measured review of their use is initiated. According to reports, a good start has been made on this with a clear commitment to separate the whole issue of methods of decision making from the provision of immunities. The following paragraphs are put forward as a contribution to carrying forward that review.

The established position
The use of ballots in trade unions has long been established, not only in law, but in the rulebooks and constitutions of unions

themselves. In addition to conducting ballots in respect of amalgamations, changes in constitution and political funds, some unions have themselves made rules for ballots covering elections, delegations, industrial action and in response to employers' pay and other offers.

The forms and organisation of those ballots have varied considerably both between unions and according to the issue in hand. Moreover, some unions have increased their use of ballots over the years and others have lessened this method of membership participation. At the very least, there has been no one fixed, universal and immutable system of balloting within the trade union movement, particularly not the 'full' postal ballot.

Ballots have never been the cornerstone of union government or democracy. Just as their use has varied between unions and over time, so too the arrangements for elections, appointments, government, participation and decision-making, have all reflected the particular circumstances, history and structure of different trade unions. What has suited one union's democratic structure has not necessarily suited another. This has been both the strength of British trade unions and has also been the basis of their resentment at having a uniform, obligatory and clearly mechanistic system forced upon them by outside bodies. The resentment is only increased when other significant organisations in British society have not been so required to accept an externally-imposed system and procedures which can even override internally agreed rules and arrangements.

It follows that trade unions have responded quite differently to ballots determined and agreed by themselves under their own procedures as against those *imposed* upon them by governments, laws or courts, by public officials, or used by employers to seek to by-pass established channels of communication and collective bargaining.

Whatever their own use of ballots, rather than endorsing a 'ballots-only' approach to union democracy, British trade unions have favoured and championed systems of internal government and democracy that combine elements of both *participative* and *representative* democracy. In trade unions all members are entitled by their continued membership to attend a wide range of union meetings including at least section or shop, workplace and branch. Typically, members take part in the election (and recall) of shop stewards and local representatives. At branch level members not only elect branch officials, discuss and decide branch policy and receive information and advice from other levels of the union, but branches are also frequently the place where attitudes to national policy and conference motions are determined and where branch delegates are elected and report back. Through their various representatives, union members are linked into collective bargaining, union government, inter-union arrangements, political parties and campaigning bodies. None of this is to say that there are no organisational or structural impediments in the way of extending democracy in unions. Obscure language, convoluted procedures, poor communications, hostility to women's participation, difficult times and places of meetings, all need constant attention. But this is a task for the unions themselves, not for other bodies, especially governments or courts. A number of unions have already tackled the issues themselves.

Underpinning this complex and sophisticated web of governmental, consultative and decision-making processes are the twin bases of *organisation* and *collectivity*. Organisation provides not only for membership and recruitment, but also for members with similar interests to be provided with a range of union services including full-time officials, legal advice and representation, information, research and finance. Collectivity for its part provides for strength in numbers which few individual members or small groups of members alone can count upon. Faced by the vast potential power of employers or the state, collectivity provides for confidence, for countervailing power and for mutual protection.

The strong case for ballots

A strong case for ballots has been made variously by trade unions themselves, political parties, employers and by commentators in the media and academic life. A number of central arguments can be outlined.

The most frequently-cited reason for advocating ballots in unions is that they will either enhance democracy or widen participation. The argument runs that, because so few trade union members actually attend the meetings where decisions are made (for whatever reasons), the use of ballots will ensure a higher turnout than recorded at workplace, mass or branch meetings.

Following closely on the first argument is the second that, as things stand, union policies and union leaderships are determined by unrepresentative minorities. According to this view, determinedly undemocratic or even subversive elements seek to benefit from the absence of their fellow trade unionists by claiming union legitimacy for their own (militant) perspectives.

A third argument (or rather hope) is closely related, namely that leaders elected or decisions taken by ballot vote will produce a greater degree of moderation and less 'militancy' in trade unions. Here the assumption appears to be that particular *methods* of election or decision-making are associated with particular *results*. There is little consistent evidence to support this assumption.

The fourth case for ballots again follows hard upon the previous argument. Other methods of union decision-making, meetings, delegations, committees and conferences are not only said to be open to the dangers of manipulation (by rhetoric or plain cheating) but, more ominously, of intimidation. Faced by the aggressive, hostile and firmly expressed views of militant and organised fellow union members, 'ordinary' rank and file members, it is said, can be either swayed or frightened into supporting decisions or candidates they would otherwise have rejected.

More fundamentally, some advocate ballots in the belief that, especially, *individual secret* ballots constitute the purest form of democracy. They believe that for unions to aspire to real democracy requires that they place this quintessentially democratic practice at the very centre of their procedures.

More practically, some support ballots in circumstances where other methods of decision-making or election are rendered impracticable because of working arrangements, employment dispersal, shift patterns, domicile or constraints of time.

From a tactical point of view, ballots are also advocated not because different leaderships or actions will follow than would have from other methods, but because of the aura of legitimacy that is said to attach to decisions based upon the ballot (especially individual secret ballots).

Finally, some advocacy of ballots rests upon the firm rejection of collectivity and collective decision-making. Block votes, mass meetings and collective affirmation and affiliation are all rejected in favour of the *individual* vote, with votes being simply aggregated rather than placed in the overall institutional and organisational context of a shop, workplace, branch or trade union. In other words, these organisational arrangements should be nothing other than shells within which individuals continue to operate, possibly irrespective of the wishes of their fellow members.

Before moving on to consider some problems with ballots, it is worth remembering how few of these arguments, so vociferously deployed in respect of trade union democracy, are applied in similarly unequivocal fashion to other British institutions. Not only do they not apply to business or voluntary organisations, to churches or clubs, but neither do they to political parties or governments, despite their adherence to secret votes in local and parliamentary elections. Certainly no major organisation in Britain is expected to take all its key decisions or elect its main leaders by constant resort to the membership of the organisation as a whole through ballots, referenda or plebiscite.

Some limitations of ballots

The strongest case against reliance on ballots has already been made. Namely, that it is naive to think that ballots alone can hope to match or replace the complex, varied and sophisticated methods of decision-making and elections already deployed in British unions. A second, powerful argument is that, rather than strengthening union organisation and collectivity (as is often assumed), reliance on ballots weakens or even seeks to weaken them. Members are not thereby encouraged to attend meetings, listen to debate, argue their case and take account of the feelings of fellow members. The strength of collectivity is thus broken down into the potential isolation of a series of individuals.

Political objections to ballots often note the enormous discretion given to leaderships, or those who frame ballot questions, by the use of ballots. Research has frequently demonstrated how the timing, wording or context of questions can have a decisive influence on ballot results. Moreover, as the Webbs noted 80 years ago, referenda usually leave the field wide open for the development of policy and attitudes by those who wield power.

In recent years, trade unionists have often complained about 'outside interference' in their internal affairs. Newspapers, television, other media of communication, political parties, hostile forces and employers, potentially all fall into this category. The fear with the use of ballots is that the influence and power of these outside bodies will be brought to bear upon trade unionists, especially where postal ballots are employed.

Objections to ballots are often also severely practical. If ballots are to be reliable they require a high degree of organisation. Membership lists and addresses need keeping up to date (much harder in some industries and occupations than others and more so where high turnover or casual work prevail). Detailed arrangements for registration of voters, for printing and distribution, for scrutineers, for checking, collection and counting, are all necessary. Every trade union can attest to the numbers of ballot forms inadvertently sent to non, former, lapsed or retired members. These problems have only been exacerbated by redundancy, unemployment, casualism and early retirement.

Similarly, ballots can often be time-consuming and cumbersome. Some decisions require fast responses and quick decisions and these can seldom be secured by ballot. Where disputes are concerned or responses to employers' offers (especially where a return to work is advocated), the ballot may entail delay, confusion and division.

Even if ballots could meet all the above objections, the final and decisive objection concerns the question of union constitutions. Union rule books normally indicate where sovereign authority lies. This may be Conference, Executive Council, Region, District, or Branch, or even a joint union or collective bargaining body, according to the matter in hand. Simply to assume that a ballot vote, however well conducted, can or should ride roughshod over these structures risks disorganisation and chaos. Strangely enough, it also throws leadership (so often advocated in other quarters of British life!) out with the bathwater.

Dispute ballots

It has become increasingly evident that the days are over of executive councils simply 'instructing' their members to strike or of reliance upon essentially *workplace* mass meetings to secure strike decisions (if indeed, those days ever existed for some unions or groups of workers). In part, this is because of the changed circumstances of the economy and labour market. It also reflects the changed level and duration of industrial action (with longer, national official strikes becoming more characteristic). Support has to be worked for, won and reinforced.

Arguments *against* ballots in these circumstances paradoxically echo some parts of the argument of those who wish to *impose* them, namely that the leadership (at whatever level) cannot afford to trust the membership (for whatever good or bad reason). Here, it must be said that open splits between leadership and membership threaten the unions and strengthen the hands of their opponents. Again, the issue cannot be whether or not ballots as such are acceptable, but who decides whether or not to hold a ballot and the form and wording that ballot must take and the method by which it is conducted.

Members and ballots

With the increased use of ballots, not only unions but also their members have become far more sophisticated in their use. It may be that employer-initiated ballots (à la Edwardes) or government-imposed ballots, did enjoy a brief period of glory, appearing to use members 'against' the unions, but once embraced within the wider panoply of unions' democratic, educational and informational procedures, it has certainly proved possible for ballots, *judiciously deployed*, to strengthen the hands of members and leaders alike.

What all of this suggests is a danger in rushing to judgement, especially to seek by statute to enshrine secret, individual ballots within trade union rule books. First, such a strategy looks to be a gross over-simplification. Secondly, it risks generating trade union hostility against the whole package if it becomes a *cause celebre*. Thirdly, if pressed ahead with, it might lead to divisions between two types of union, the 'certified' and the 'non-certified', each with different rights and financial status, and it will be remembered what happened to a similar arrangement under the 1971 Industrial Relations Act. Fourthly, such a statutory requirement invites recalcitrant union members to resort to the courts where they consider a union has failed to uphold its own (statutorily required) rules. The National Union of Mineworkers' case and its treatment is, of course, instructive in this regard.

What If Labour Is Not Elected?

In conclusion, serious thought needs to be given to what (if anything) the ideas and perspective outlined in this paper can contribute in the event of Labour not being elected to government in the next general election. Of course, it has to be said that the *aim* of the approach outlined here is to contribute towards the election of a government persuaded of its merits. However, if such a government is not elected, despite the detailed attention given earlier to the creation of a powerful and influential new public body, the general perspective advocated can *still* be worked for by the trade unions and their supporters. Indeed, many of the initiatives proposed depend heavily upon the voluntary self-activity and campaigns of the unions (and some managers) and are not merely to be triggered by legal or public policy prior actions.

It was earlier suggested that significant advances in trade unionism and collective bargaining have been based not only on active public support and advocacy, but also upon the actions and strength of workers and their own organisations. In the event of an absence of public support, the next phase of union development and the extension of workers' rights will depend almost exclusively upon that second side of the dialectic.

References

1.. TUC. *Industrial Relations Legislation: a TUC Consultative Document* (London: TUC, January 1986).

2. See, for example, *The Guardian*, 24.6.86. Robert Taylor, writing in *The Observer* on 29.6.86, went even further, suggesting the inclusion of sanctions against unions not yet in the TUC Labour Party Liaison Committee draft paper.

3. See, for example, William McCarthy, *Freedom at Work: Towards the Reform of Tory Employment Laws*. Fabian Society Pamphlet No. 508, (London: Fabian Society, November 1985). John Edmonds, Chapter 8. See also the debates held by the Haldane Society and reported in its *Employment Law Bulletin*. J. Torode, "The rights that could turn out to be wrong for the trade unions", *The Guardian*, 7.1.86.

4. See Appendix 1 for details of employment changes in Britain since the Second World War. See also J. Edmonds *loc. cit.*

5. See Appendix 2 for the long-term trends in unemployment and for recent forecasts in employment.

6. See J. Atkinson and D. Gregory, "A flexible future: Britain's dual labour force", *Marxism Today*, April 1986, pp.12-17 and J. Atkinson, "Flexibility, Uncertainty and Manpower Management", *IMS Report*, No. 89, September 1984.

7. C. Johnson, *A Giant's Strength: some thoughts on the constitutional and the legal position of trade unions in England* (London: Inns of Court Conservative and Unionist Society, June 1958) p.14.

8. For a more detailed analysis see J. McIlroy, "Police and Pickets: the Law against the Miners" in H. Beynon (ed.) *Digging Deeper: Issues in the Miners' Strike* (London: Verso, 1985) pp.101-122.

9. See, for example, R. Lewis, P. Davies and B. Wedderburn, *Industrial Relations Law and the Conservative Government* Fabian Trade Union Special (London: NCCL, October 1979).

10. See Roy Lewis (ed.) *Labour Law in Britain* (Oxford: Basil Blackwell, 1986) p.36. Lewis has in mind legislative provision for equal rights at work.

11. *Annual Report* of the Certification Officer, 1985 (London: HMSO, 1985).

12. See, for example, I. Linn, *Single Union Deals* (Barnsley, Northern College and TGWU, 1986).

13. E. Batstone, *Working Order* (Oxford, Basil Blackwell, 1984) pp.294-295. Bain and Price also warn against precipitate apocalyptic predictions "In spite of the unfavourable environment in which the trade union movement now finds itself, however, it is unlikely to lose all the faith which it achieved during the 'decade' of growth ... union recognition was greatly extended and deepened during the 1970's, with the result that trade unionism and the collective bargaining which makes it possible are now more deeply embedded in the management process than ever before. This greater degree of union recognition is likely to act as a ratchet which will prevent union membership slipping away on a scale which occurred, for example, during the mass unemployment of the inter-war years.
R. Price and G.S. Bain "Union Growth in Britain: Retrospect and Prospect", *British Journal of Industrial Relations* Vol. XXI, No. 1, March, 1983, p.63.

14. *loc. cit.* p.18.

15. See, for example, P. Brannen *et al*, *The Worker Directors* (London: Hutchinson, 1976), and E. Batstone, A. Ferner and M. Terry *Workers on the Board* (Oxford: Basil Blackwell, 1983).

16. P. Cressey and J. McInnes *Industrial Democracy on Theories of Power and Control*

in the Workplace (Glasgow: University of Glasgow, Centre for Research in Industrial Democracy, October 1980).

17.   *Ibid.* p.25.
18.   See Huw Beynon and Terry Austrin, *Global Outpost: The Working Class Experience of Big Business in the North East of England 1964-1979* (Durham: Department of Sociology, n.d.).
19.   TUC, *TUC Strategy*, TUC Consultative Document, March 1984.
20.   Otto Kahn-Freund, *Labour and the Law* (London: Stevens, 1972)/
21.   For more details, see Bain and Price *loc. cit.*
22.   *loc. cit.*
23.   See, for example, the idea "floated" in *The Observer, loc. cit.* 29.6.86.

Appendix 1

The Changing British Labour Force 1948-1984
in Selected Industries (000's)

	1948	1968	Change 48-68	1979	Change 69-79	1984 (June)	Change 79-84
Chemicals	401.0	474.6	+73.6	490.5	+15.9	441.2	−49.3
Metals and Eng.	3,514.4	4,249.8	+735.4	3,809.4	−440.4	2810.9	−998.5
Cotton and Man-Made Fibres	350.1	180.6	−169.5	114.1	−66.5	89.8	−24.3
Coal Mining	800.1	443.8	−356.3	306.6	−137.2	224.9	−81.7
Electricity	157.4	242.3	+84.9	179.9	−62.4	155.7	−24.2
Water	29.3	47.5	+18.2	66.2	+18.7	65.1	−1.1
National Govt	709.1	602.7	−106.4	639.5	+36.8	620.3	−19.2
Local Govt and Education	1,241.2	2,221.2	+980.0	2,879.9	+658.7	2880.7	+0.8
Railways	535.3	274.5	−260.8	208.9	−65.6	187.4	−21.5
Health Services	521.9	976.3	+454.4	1,317.9	+341.6	1295.0	−22.9

Appendix 2

UK Unemployment and Vacancies 1965-84 (000's)

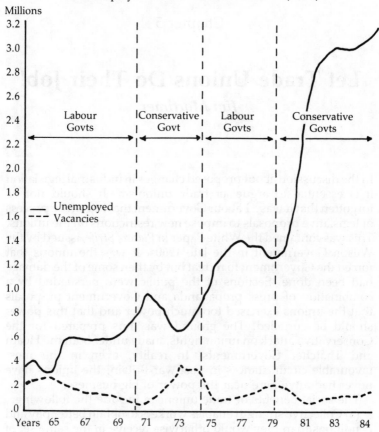

Chapter 5

Let Trade Unions Do Their Job!
Jim Mortimer

In the discussion about proposed changes in industrial legislation it is essential to argue *for* trade unionism. It should not be forgotten that it was a Labour Government that began the process of legislative proposals to impose new restrictions on the unions. This was contained the White Paper *In Place of Strife*, issued by the Wilson Government in the late 1960s. It was the unions that forced the Government to retreat but by then some of the damage had been done. Sections of the public were persuaded by a combination of press propaganda and Government proposals that the unions exercised too much power and that this power should be curtailed. The ground was thus prepared for the Conservative attack on union rights, made under both the Heath and Thatcher Governments. In reality, even in the most favourable circumstances in post-war Britain, the unions have never had anywhere near the power of big business.

The social benefits of trade unionism include the following:

(a) Collective strength enables workers to obtain better pay and conditions than they would otherwise receive in the same set of economic and employment circumstances.

(b) Collective strength enables workers to join in the determination of their pay and conditions and provides protection against arbitrary acts of injustice in their employment. Thus trade unionism is an essential democratic countervailing influence against the unilateral power of employers. It helps to redress the imbalance of the employment relationship between a more powerful employer and a weaker individual employee.

(c) Collective organisation enables workers to reach a considered and collective view on the conduct of the industry or service in which they work, and sometimes to influence decisions.

(d) Collective organisation enables workers to exert a social and political influence on all issues of concern to the interests of working people, e.g. employment policy, social services, training and education, safety at work, retirement and pensions, and health care.

In the legitimate concern to extend legal protection for individual employment rights care should be taken not to give the impression that individual rights are seen as an alternative to the full protection of collective trade union rights. Nor should the impression be given, even though this is not the intention, that the emphasis is being placed on individual rights because it might be more difficult to argue for collective rights, given the hostility of most of the press. The individual interests of workers are served not only by individual employment rights but above all by collective organisation and strength.

What a Labour Government Should Do

The next Labour Government should commit itself to the total repeal of the Conservative Government's two Employment Acts and the Trade Union Act. It should also commit itself to introduce a new Fair Wages Resolution, to extend the powers of Wages Councils to help lower paid workers, to restore schedule II of the Employment Protection Act which provided unilateral arbitration in certain defined circumstances, to abolish notional strike pay when calculating social security payments to the dependents of workers involved in disputes, and to introduce a national minimum wage. The Government should give clear notice that it intends to consult the TUC at every stage. Any exceptional provisions in the repealed legislation to protect trade unionism should be embodied in new legislation. It should not be used to avoid the total repeal of the Conservative legislation. Total repeal will demonstrate to the British people and to the labour movement the Labour Party's commitment to restore trade union rights and the Party's unequivocal support for trade unionism. The other measures suggested above will provide a framework for helping to tackle low pay.

Some of the essential collective rights for trade unionists are as follows:

(a) The right to organise.

(b) The right to bargain collectively.

(c) The right to strike and to take employment action short of a strike.

(d) The right to picket in a dispute. This right should embrace both the right peacefully to persuade and the right peacefully to demonstrate.

(e) The right to seek and to give solidarity in disputes, including strike action and the 'blacking' of work.

(f) The right of unions to determine their own decision-making processes and to have their affairs conducted in accordance with their own rule books, providing always that both union and members have access to the courts for protection of property, funds and entitlements.

Not one of these rights is today adequately protected by British law.

The Employment Protection Act gives legal protection against the dismissal of workers on grounds of trade union membership. It is of some help, but real protection comes not from law but from trade union strength. It is still possible for employers to discriminate against active trade unionists when recruiting employees. It has also been possible for the National Coal Board to refuse to re-employ miners who were dismissed during the last national strike despite decisions by industrial tribunals that they were unfairly dismissed, and despite the triviality of alleged offences in certain other cases. A Labour Government should direct British Coal to re-employ immediately all miners who have won their cases at tribunals and to review, together with the National Union of Mineworkers (NUM), all other cases. This would help to set a new standard for public policy against the victimisation of trade unionists. It would influence other industries and services. British Coal and all nationalised industries should also be directed not in any way to encourage breakaway unions. The members of the Union of Democratic Mineworkers (UDM) should be encouraged to return to the NUM. If they do not do so, they should not be given any privileges over members of the NUM.

To uphold the right to bargain collectively (i.e. the right of trade union recognition) presents the most difficult legislative problem for a Labour Government. The experience of the statutory recognition procedures under the Employment Protection Act was not encouraging. Statutory recognition procedures are likely to involve detailed requirements for enquiry, the ascertainment of workers' opinions, consultation with all concerned, including employers, the determination of negotiating group boundaries, and, unfortunately, adjudication between the claims of competing unions. The opportunities for legal protests, procrastination and obstruction are almost limitless and the intervention of the courts on a wide scale probably inevitable. Moreover, a statutory procedure is likely to run into conflict with the procedures of the TUC for resolving disputes between unions.

The right of recognition should belong to any group of trade unionists who want it, providing that the union which is seeking recognition is not intruding into the legitimate sphere of influence of another union as understood under the TUC disputes procedure. In other words, providing a union is not raiding another union's legitimate sphere of influence, recognition should not depend on majority support (as in the USA) or even on any required level of minority support. To impose such a requirement is to deny the trade union right of those who want it. There is nothing in the International Labour Organization (ILO) Conventions on the right to organise or the right to bargain collectively which justifies or requires a given level of membership for collective bargaining. The point can be illustrated by the example of the Tolpuddle Martyrs. They did not represent a majority of workers. Nevertheless, they should have been given the right to make representations in their own interests. Members should have representational rights through their own union, though, of course, their collective strength will be weak if the union represents only a small minority of the eligible workers.

The importance of the concept of a union's legitimate sphere of influence for recognition purposes underlines the need to ensure that the trade union movement itself regulates relationships between unions, develops solidarity and eliminates 'raiding' for membership. These are not matters for the courts. A sphere of influence, as TUC experience has demonstrated, cannot be defined rigidly in advance or determined for all time. It takes account of history, inter-union relationships, success or lack of success in organising efforts, employers' resistance, industrial development and technological change, and changes in trade union structure, including amalgamations. It is a flexible and sophisticated concept.

It is difficult to construct a legal framework for the right to bargain collectively without introducing very considerable legal hazards. Probably the most effective way for a Labour Government to help recognition would be by:

First, a declaration of policy in favour of trade union recognition. This would help to create a favourable climate of opinion.

Secondly, the readiness of all ministers, in consultation with the TUC, to use their influence in favour of trade union recognition in all cases where firms receive public contracts or any kind of public financial assistance. In this area voluntary influence is usually more appropriate than statutory penalties.

Thirdly, removing legal curtailments on solidarity action, including solidarity affecting public services. (This has been an effective instrument in Sweden, e.g. recognition was gained at IBM in contrast to other countries, including Britain, where IBM have successfully resisted recognition.)

Fourthly, encouraging the Advisory, Conciliation and Arbitration Service (ACAS) to act in pursuit of its obligation under the Employment Protection Act to promote collective bargaining and to use fully the machinery of conciliation and, if necessary, enquiry for this purpose.

The right to strike is essential for effective trade unionism. This is not to argue that strike action is the only way to resolve problems. Indeed, the overwhelming majority of issues can and should be resolved by negotiations, conducted in accordance with good negotiating procedures. Good procedures should permit any issue to be raised which is of concern to either side, should provide for the first stage of negotiations to be conducted expeditiously at the workplace, should provide for trade union workplace representation, should provide facilities for effective trade union functioning at the workplace, should provide for the disclosure of information to assist collective bargaining, and should require that changes are not imposed unilaterally without agreement or unless the negotiating machinery has been exhausted.

'Rights' or 'Immunities'?

The question has to be asked as to whether the right to strike can best be protected by a positive right embodied in legislation or by a legal immunity. This is not a great issue of principle. Neither does either alternative offer a guarantee against future erosion. The criterion as to which is preferable relates only to the protection which either is likely to offer.

The problem with a positive right to strike is that, with the continued existence of the common law, it invites a circumscribing definition either by legislation or by judicial interpretation. Thus, for example, to what kind of dispute should it apply? If it is to an industrial dispute only, then that has to be defined. Should the strike be protected whether or not it is in breach of employment contracts? Is the giving of strike notice sufficient to discharge the contract? Should provision be made for the suspension of employment contracts so as to protect occupational pension rights? Should the strike be protected if it causes loss because of the breach of contracts other than employment contracts? Should it be protected if it interferes with trade, business or commerce which is not party to the dispute, or causes personal inconvenience or loss? Is the threat of strike action in certain circumstances to be regarded as intimidatory? Has the strike been called in accordance with the rules of the union, is it in breach of the negotiating procedure, has a ballot been conducted, among whom was the ballot taken, was the question on the ballot 'fair', and was the ballot authorised by the union? Have there been any 'unfair' practices? The list is endless. These are not hypothetical questions. They are to be found in trade union legal history. If these questions are not answered in the positive rights legislation it is probable that stage by stage the judges will provide their own answers, and most of the answers will not be in the direction desired by the unions and the wider labour movement.

It needs to be repeated that a legal immunity is not a guarantee against new liabilities being invented by the judiciary. The common law, like the blue of the sky, has no permanent boundaries. It is what the judges say it is and they extend it from time to time. They discover or invent new liabilities.

It can, however, be argued that an immunity is more likely to deter adverse judicial intervention than a positive right. The immunity would have to say something to the effect that no court should entertain any legal action which arose only from a breach of contract, whether of employment or otherwise, interference with trade, business or commerce, personal inconvenience or loss, caused as a result of a strike or employment action short of a strike, or the threat of such action, taken in pursuit of a dispute affecting the employment relationship. The precise wording would, of course, be a matter for lawyers and would have to take account of experience with previous immunities embodied in trade union legislation. The labour movement should consider extending the existing definition of a 'trade dispute' to cover all disputes in which unions might become involved, e.g. a boycott of South African goods.

Picketing and Solidarity Action

The right to picket can best be upheld by a positive right. Unfortunately, it has been undermined in the recent past by court decisions which appear to have given legal effect to particular interpretations of voluntary codes of practice, suggesting a limit to the number of pickets, and to the extensive use of police powers which have subsequently been sanctioned by the courts.

The positive right to picket should assert not only the right of citizens to seek to persuade peacefully other citizens at their place of work to take some form of employment action as a means of support in a dispute, but also the right peacefully to demonstrate in the same cause. The obligation of the police should be to protect the rights of all citizens, including those at work, pickets and demonstrators, and to consult with representatives of all concerned with a view to making this obligation effective. Thus the police would seek to protect:

(a) The right of citizens peacefully to go about their business.

(b) The right of citizens peacefully to picket and demonstrate in a dispute. This would involve consultation about means of communicating information, e.g. halting lorries in police presence.

(c) The right of citizens not to have their domestic lives disrupted by a police presence in their streets designed to protect the transport of lorries engaged in breaking a strike. Citizens should be consulted and their interests should not be subordinated to those who are seeking to break a strike. There should be a fair balance of the interests of all citizens.

One of the most vital requirements is to restore to trade unionists the right to seek and to give solidarity in disputes. This right has been virtually outlawed by the Conservative Government. Public service workers should not be subject to special legal restrictions. This is not to suggest that they should be drawn into more and more disputes. Their own caution will provide a safeguard. But in recognition disputes in particular employers should not be entitled to legal protection against solidarity action by public service workers whilst denying recognition to their own workers, e.g. Grunwick.

Union Decision-making

Unions are entitled to shape their own decision-making processes. Article 3 of the ILO Convention, no.87, 'Freedom of Association', reads:

"Workers' and employers' organisations shall have the right to draw up their constitutions and rules, to elect their representatives in full freedom, to organise their administration and activities and to formulate their programmes.

The public authorities shall refrain from any interference which would restrict this right or impede the lawful exercise thereof."

For the state to decide how decisions are to be made by unions, e.g. on strikes, or how officials should be elected, whether by ballot, or by election at the annual conference or by the executive committee, is an infringement of freedom of association. It should have no place in industrial relations legislation. There has never been uniformity of practice in the British trade union movement and no government is entitled to impose uniformity on trade unionists. Article 8 of the ILO Convention, no.87, concerning freedom of association and protection of the right to organise, states that whilst workers' and employers' organisations must respect the law of the land, the law must not impair the guarantees provided in the Convention. One of the most important of these guarantees is that workers' and employers' organisations have the right to draw up their own rules and to organise their own administration.

The ILO Convention on freedom of association envisages that workers' and employers' organisations may acquire a legal personality. This is usually required for protection of property and funds and for dealing with questions that arise therefrom. In Britain unions should be able to continue to protect their property and funds, but, as the ILO Convention recognises, this acquisition of a legal personality for certain limited purposes should not be subject to conditions which impair or limit the application of trade union rights. Trade unions are essentially voluntary bodies. Trade union structure and the varied methods of making decisions are matters for trade unionists themselves. It is not for the state to dictate. This is the essence of trade union independence from interference by the state.

It follows from this that proposals, whether from within the labour movement or from opponents, which seek to impose legal requirements for balloting for strikes, trade union recognition, or the election of representatives should be opposed. Ballots have always occupied an important place in trade union democracy. But it is for the membership to decide through the rule book when and how ballots should be held. Moreover, ballots are not the total substance of trade union democracy. Informed discussion when decisions are being reached is vital. This necessitates meetings and conferences. A system of representative democracy, with delegates and with representatives carrying executive responsibility, is more likely to be an indication of democratic maturity than the corruption of power. Some of the current pressure for ballots — as in the Conservative Party — comes from people who wish to belittle the influence of active trade unionists, who give no weight to other important aspects of trade union democracy and who wish to strengthen the influence of a hostile press on the decision-making processes of trade unions.

The adoption of any proposal, which directly or indirectly, made strike ballots compulsory would lay a legal minefield which the labour movement would come to regret. There is a variety of circumstances in which in real life workers may take immediate strike action but where the responsibility for precipitating the dispute lies elsewhere. What of strikes that take place because an employer has made unilateral changes that are likely to affect piece-work earnings? Immediate stoppages may also take place because of particularly bad conditions on an exposed site, or because of the victimisation of a trade unionist. If ballots were to be imposed, directly or indirectly, by law, penalties would have to be imposed if an infringement took place. On whom would the penalty be imposed? Would it be on individual workers or on the union? New liabilities would be created which would help to create a sense of injustice and would lead to controversy.

Employment Rights
Much has been written elsewhere about upholding and extending individual employment rights, e.g. unfair dismissal. Nothing has been said about these issues in this chapter, not because they are unimportant, but because there is more likely to be agreement about them. It needs to be borne in mind, however, that individual statutory employment rights are not a panacea and they are not a substitute for trade unionism. Unfortunately, as the conciliation experience of ACAS showed, some workers tend to regard the statutory process as a *substitute* for trade unionism. Statutory rights are a relevant *supplement* to trade unionism and they have a 'civilising' effect on some more difficult employers.

One important area for extending employment rights is to extend to unions the right to claim facilities at workplace level for trade union functions. This should include meeting facilities, notice-boards, and facilities for literature distribution, subscription collection, and balloting. It might be preferable to embody these rights in a Code of Practice, supplemented by voluntary conciliation through ACAS and an affirmation in a revised Fair Wages Resolution for application in all public contracts and in all firms receiving any kind of public financial assistance. Ministerial pressures could also be helpful. The alternative of embodying these rights in law might invite judicial intervention and limitation by interpretation. This, however, should be open to discussion. The objective would be to achieve effectiveness without a succession of legal problems.

Chapter 6

Industrial Democracy and Socialist Priorities

John Hughes

Introduction

This chapter attempts no more than a sketch. It seeks to outline some of the concepts required if we are to establish constructive links between a number of the key objectives of a future Labour Government and a significant move towards industrial democracy. It approaches the latter, industrial democracy, primarily in the sense of extending collective influence by workers and their representatives over 'strategic' decisions by enterprises (private and public) over development, resource use, business organisation, etc. (This is not to deny the significance of other aspects of industrial democracy, such as individual workers' rights).

From this point of view, it would be quite inadequate to treat the current discussion of Labour Law as if it centred merely on the task of removing the repressive structure of law generated by the Thatcher Government. The massive collapse of both employment and trade union ability to resist mass displacement of labour (e.g. one quarter of the manufacturing labour force) in the early 1980s did not result from new labour laws; nor did the massive shifts in the 'frontier of control' within plants. (Though the new labour laws could be seen as designed to impede cumulatively any major restoration of trade union functions.) The point is that the previous Labour Government had failed to bequeath a framework of collective rights *vis-a-vis* the development and displacement processes of conglomerate enterprise; we had not even secured the degree of explicit protection of employment and participation in enterprise strategy by workers' representatives found in some continental European practice. Looking back at the 1970s, it is a nice question whether we could be said to have lost battles to establish a relevant industrial democracy, or whether we had largely been fighting the wrong battles in the wrong terms. What *is* certain is the importance of establishing a working alliance between a future Labour Government, trade unions, and working people generally, not simply about new legislation, but about the combined constructive force that can be brought to bear after such legislation to secure work and development in the United Kingdom.

Looking Back — The 1970s

The first comment is an attempt to take a charitable view of the confused slogans and objectives surrounding industrial democracy in the 1970s. Whatever the weakness of the leading ideas and policies that were advocated, they had one common characteristic. They would, to a greater or lesser extent, have done something to overcome the most serious weakness in trade union organisation, namely the almost total failure to establish or maintain coherent joint organisation, with developing and significant functions, at the level of large scale conglomerate companies. All the notions that were developed could be seen as designed to jolt trade union organisation towards that degree of coherence, by offering major functions that could not otherwise be taken up. This is a point that we cannot afford to neglect; we cannot hide from the reality of the persistent and widespread weaknesses of trade union organisation (in any combined and adequately serviced sense) at the level of the major conglomerate enterprises. And one touchstone in testing ideas that are put forward on industrial democracy is simply to ask what would be achieved in terms of a leap forward in union organisational effectiveness at corporate level.

Let us remind ourselves briefly of the main panaceas that were canvassed in the 1970s. Firstly, there was emphasis on *Planning Agreements*. In principle, we should not deride this, since the idea of linking up the priorities of government supported programmes of industrial development with trade union functions is important. In practice, the idea was weak in every direction. The 'consultative' role of trade unions was a weak and ill-defined formula. Companies had little difficulty (encouraged in this by the Confederation of British Industry) in talking out indefinitely the Departmental attempts to sign them up for an overall Agreement. This was particularly likely to happen because the *actual* processes of negotiating selective industrial aid were located around *particular* company projects of investment, not complete development strategies. Neither the planning process nor the functional capacity of the unions were in tune with the heady rhetoric. True, the unions were located in the tripartite industrial committees of so-called Industrial Strategy; but these committees were given virtually no decision-making role, and, in the main, trade union involvement was steered away from the real — and very large scale and influential — negotiating over funding, etc. that was going on between government and companies, or divisions of companies.

Secondly, there were arguments about '*workers on the Board*' and the Bullock Committee. Looking back, it was ironic that the Trade Union Congress took up proposals on the involvement of workers' representatives in the direction of companies that were adapted from European Commission proposals, and this at a time when the official TUC policy was still opposed to UK membership of the Common Market. This approach went too far in the direction of *disconnecting* the emphasised form of enterprise level 'industrial democracy' from the remainder of union structures and functions already developed, or capable of being developed, inside the enterprise; it disconnected the issue also from other aspects of the public accountability of large scale firms. Instead, it posed — without fully resolving — awkward questions as to the accountability of the proposed worker directors.

Thirdly, there were the attempts to pursue participation in occupational pension schemes through the proposal that the recognised trade unions should be able to claim 50 per cent of the seats of all bodies concerned with the general management of occupational pension schemes. While this was close to existing practice in some nationalised industries, it would have generated an important joint-union function across much of the private sector (not least because a careful balance of representation of interests might be involved). But here too, the initiative was not linked to a wider review of the social responsibilities and accountability of trustees and funds, connecting the privileged tax position of such funds with the pressing needs of UK-based industrial and commercial development.

We are left with the sense of a series of stabs at the issue, substantially disconnected from each other and not linked up in any convincing way with wider initiatives in economic development and accountability. Perhaps what was still lacking was an appreciationof the severity of the crisis of development and employment. Besides, too many of the actors were caught up in short run pressures (not least around the handling of the 'social contract').

Criteria for an Industrial Democracy Programme

There must be a high degree of subjectivity involved in asserting the elements that would be desirable in a future programme of initiatives on industrial democracy. On the other hand, putting forward specific proposals without identifying key tests of relevance and urgency that they should meet is to return to the trap of the 1970s.

The major elements in the extension of industrial democracy should be accessible to public as well as to private sector workers and trade unions. Locating the rights, initiatives and responsibilities involved only within commercial enterprise must give the appearance of discriminating over workers' rights. The issue is the more important since workers in the public services have all too often in the last two decades found themselves at the receiving end of arbitrary decision-making and resource allocation by government. The case for opening up the role of workers' representatives in the development of public services is all the more evident since,

(a) constraints on total resources in relation to pressing social needs invite the initiative and active co-operation of the workers involved; and

(b) more of the central government funding made available is likely to be selective and conditional in its provision. It makes sense to be thinking of 'planning agreements' affecting substantial parts of the public service area.

The extension of industrial democracy should not be disconnected from but rather built on to existing effective industrial relations practices and structures. Not all current practice is an exercise in total alienation. This means that we should be particularly interested in experiment and in functionally relevant variety. For that reason, the processes of industrial democracy should not be fitted into a single strait-jacket.

We should look to a cumulative combination of functions, rights, and opportunities to push us towards qualitative changes in organisation and the nature of working practice. We need to remember that the legacy of the Thatcher Government is not only an unresolved economic development crisis (exemplified by unprecedented structural unemployment) but also greatly intensified *inequality* in every dimension of working and social life. An isolated gesture towards wider participation and equality of esteem is not going to move the old cultures of hierarchy and discrimination.

Wherever possible, the structures of industrial democracy should carry a direct role in the allocation of real resources — including financial choices — and should be backed up by relevant and specialised facilities. Not least this requirement is true of human investment and development programmes.

Industrial democracy as the recognition and extension of the rights and opportunities of specific groups needs to develop within frameworks and guidelines that recognise wider social and economic responsibilities and priorities. In advancing the rights of those *in* work, we have an obligation to ensure that the forms and conditions of this assist those *out* of work. Industrial democracy generates particular styles of accountability, but it should be linked with wider social accountability. For instance, industrial democracy involves workers and their representatives in aspects of the entrepreneurial management of production processes; but this 'trustee' role needs to operate within frameworks that use the wider rationality of social accounting — recognising and signalling social benefits and costs as well as narrowly commercial costs and revenues. Industrial democracy will also mean the development of 'trustee' roles in management of financial assets, and of various forms of social funds; the same principle applies.

The industrial democracy programme will need to be more socialist than syndicalist, but it expresses the urgency of offering socialism from below, enabling, supporting a wider sharing of power and resources, participative rather than hierarchical. The necessity of the socialist elements springs in part from the crucial role of legislation, but perhaps even more from the continuing need to *enable* initiatives to go ahead in a socially responsible way. We have already argued the importance of signalling to enterprises *social* costs and benefits (e.g. through taxes, levies, rebates, conditional funding). We should add the urgency of fighting *against* acute patterns of discrimination in employment (part-timers; casualised labour; ethnic and sex discrimination) and *for* the creation of additional productive jobs. Hence the cultural role of the state; but this is a socialising state rather than the old-style state socialism. But it would need to be a genuine *alliance* between the socialising state and syndicalist energy. One test would be that public ownership is not elevated to a deified category and then used to circumscribe the rights and initiatives of public sector workers. Another test would be that the state does not insist on one uniform prescription for industrial democracy (a contradiction in any case to the notion of encouraging the self-determination of workers), but instead offers and encourages a range of opportunities for social learning and responsibility in employment.

The measures taken to extend industrial democracy should in particular encourage (by generating important trade union functions) more coherent joint trade union liaison, organisation, and servicing, across the large conglomerate enterprise. In practice this is likely to require a good deal of patient effort by the TUC and its industrial committees; this at least is something that could — and should — start *now*, not only in its own right as an organisational priority but so that future opportunities can be taken up swiftly and effectively.

Industrial Democracy: What Type of Programme?
To be effective the programme has to build up from two related initiatives. Firstly, there have, of course, to be enterprise-wide structures capable of handling joint participation on strategic issues of business operation and development; this means that the enterprises themselves have to be required to develop such structures where their workers and trade unions want them. But, secondly, the state has to generate new elements of public accountability over major aspects of business function, and new patterns of control over allocation of financial resources, which call for active exercise of responsibility and function by workers' representatives; that is, the state creates a series of crucial functions which organised workers in the large enterprises will reach out to. *The test of credibility for proposals on industrial democracy is that they provide for the interlocking and mutual reinforcement of these two elements.*

Let us try to envisage what is called for by way of rights and joint structures at enterprise level. The 'enterprise' may of course be a public one (or a public service) as well as the privately owned one, that past discussions have concentrated on. We need a statute that will steer us in the following ways.

— In general terms the requirement will be to establish an enterprise-wide 'Participation Agreement' between management and representatives of the workforce.

— There will have to be some size (of enterprise labour force) criterion and some timetable. Size might be initially (as even the CBI suggested in the mid 1970s) those firms and public services with 2,000 plus employees; but this should be lowered subsequently. Since time is not on our side, the timetable should be brisk, otherwise our future government could be half-way through its period of office before democratic participation was the order of the day. (Doubtless this was why the CBI thought four years a suitable suggestion when it gave evidence to the Bullock Committee). Suppose we say within 12 months of a formal request from the workers concerned.

— The trigger? Let us assume that management is required to establish such agreements if requested by trade union organisations representing a significant proportion of the labour force; if there is a challenge on the adequacy of such representative capacity, that is something that ACAS might be required to resolve.

— The strategic issues to be handled by such Agreements would need spelling out (in an ACAS code?); one would expect discussion of take-overs and de-vestment; major investment programmes; in general, prior consultation on major decisions affecting the labour force; the business situation together with forward operating objectives (and constraints); enterprise commitments to research and to training. But, in addition, the Agreements should be related carefully to existing collective bargaining agreements (so as to enhance them rather than to undermine), and should review and relate to the framework of participation in the enterprise at key 'operating' levels, such as product divisions, regions, and plants.

— The Agreements would need to provide the necessary resources and facilities to enable workers' representatives to exercise their role efficiently, with access to data and specialist advice.

— If there is failure to reach an Agreement within the specified time-scale, then either side should be able to resort to ACAS services for conciliation or an arbitrated solution. Such an arbitrated solution would operate for a specified period, unless modified by agreement of the parties.

The outline so far offered does not present too many stumbling blocks. The use of ACAS, rather than some specially created agency for turning us all into industrial democrats, is proposed to emphasis the degree of connection and continuity required with existing bargained agreements and procedures. Besides, it seems better to build on the best available, and experienced, conciliation and arbitration. There would be a degree of discretion on such things as recourse to ballots of workers to trigger the whole process or legitimate the actual Agreement that emerges.

There are, however, a number of critical questions still unresolved so far as companies are concerned. these particularly relate to the extent and role of 'worker directors', and might be tackled (a) by further but connected developments in company law, as well as (b) by staging this aspect after the main structures of Participation Agreements are in place and operating effectively. Company law is involved since it may well be right to open up on a wide scale the adoption of 'two-tier' boards, one of executive direction and the other 'supervisory'. It would be natural — not least if we are *also* asking for more responsible, interventionist, and 'social' ownership influence to be exerted by pension funds — for a development of 'supervisory' boards with extensive rights and responsibilities to involve membership made up of both major stakeholder (e.g. election by institutional shareholders) and nominees of the enterprise's workforce. In that case the social role of *inter alia* trade union trustees in pension funds holding a stake in the enterprise would connect with the acceptance of rights and responsibilities of trade unionists representing employees in the enterprise concerned. It is difficult to understand why the proceedings of the Bullock Committee did not bring forward the issue of shareholder representation but instead left it in the background and still retained centre stage a largely unreformed managerialism. Again, if a 'unitary' board is retained, then we should be discussing, in terms of company law, an enhanced role for 'non-executive directors', and could envisage these coming from both employee interests and stakeholder interests. All this points to encouragement of a degree of experiment, but governed by the exercise of pressure to move away from the largely unaccountable managerialism of the present. As to *process*, perhaps the leading joint committee established by enterprise Participation Agreements could be required by some due date to formulate proposals for participation in the direction and supervision of the company, and for the ways in which that would connect with reporting and accountability to workers and shareholders respectively. If there is disagreement then, again, ACAS could play a role and, again, it would be natural to seek employee endorsement through ballot.

Another critical question left unresolved as yet in the discussion of participation in the directing role of companies is the multi-national dimension. Are we really assuming that we can 'capture' from a single national base the global direction of multinational enterprises whose headquarters and registration happen to be in the United Kingdom? European Community development of the concept of 'Euro-company' structures is worth further consideration.

Adaptation of requirements for participation such as those outlined above to the *public* sector has so far also been inadequately considered. It was noticeable in the 1970s that 'Bullock' type experiments were pursued by particular nationalised industries. They left the uncomfortable feeling that they were exercises in legitimating a highly centralised and hierarchical managerial system, reinforcing the 'top down' structures that were left unchanged; what was needed instead was much more emphasis on opening up areas of genuine initiative and choice at operational level. We should in our public services be seizing the opportunity to encourage more variety in organisational forms (e.g. we could do with some powerful further and higher educational consortia instead of being constrained by existing structures), and more ways of bringing community as well as employee interests to bear on objectives and their fulfilment.

Planning, Accountability, and Worker Participation

It is time to turn to the crucial importance of the next Labour administration bringing forward a whole range of *key issues* and of associated *funding* in ways that propel enterprises (and public services) into far more planned, accountable, and participative development activity than would emerge otherwise. Here all that is attempted is to provide the flavour of what should be done. In principle what is to be aimed at is to correct the 'signalling' of the unreformed market economy so that more of the time enterprise management is pursuing commercial goals within patterns of cost and patterns of revenue and demand that include (unavoidably) wider social, and not least UK developmental, costs and benefits. To put it most simply, unreformed elements of market power and neglect of social interests have to be challenged through a combination of stick and carrot; stronger public accountability and enforcement of minimum standards on the one hand, more financial and other inducements to co-operate actively in development on the other. And in all this, a development of institutional forms and requirements that foster the constructive role of trade unions and work groups.

Let us give some examples of what could be involved, and how it could galvanise the enhanced and extending elements of industrial democracy to develop within a wider framework of collective and social responsibilities (instead of commercialised enterprise narrowness). Remember it would be the *cumulative* significance of the functions and openings generated that would be most important in shifting the old, alienated industrial cultures.

(a) *Human investment and training* (abysmally neglected across most of employment today). This could be approached by a levy on *all* enterprises, not payroll related since that might discourage employment, but based on *value added*. Such a levy would signal the sheer social necessity (for economic survival) of a more dynamic and efficient use of labour in all its forms and skills. It would need to be in the £1 billion to £2 billion *per annum* range initially, but could be stepped up and would be reinforced by central government funding of training and higher education (particularly within its continuing education form). Of course, such large funds would then be used to stimulate and finance much more powerful development of work-related education and training than now, *and* powerful provision for servicing and developing the competence of all those participating in industrial democracy. The most progressive enterprises would *gain* considerably and be financially supported as they step up their 'human investment', but the requirement would be shared responsibility for designing and operating the activity and resources involved and the new partnerships with the educational sector. All large enterprises would be required to develop forward labour force/skill/work organisation plans in this context.

(b) The previous paragraph can be repeated with the key words *research and development* in place of training (obviously the two react directly on each other). The levy on value added can serve the two-fold purpose of funding a major step forward in support for research and training. Empirical study suggests that high and effective research and development, together with high and improving (labour) skill endowment are crucial to long run export performance; so such an approach signals the priorities of economic survival. There is no 'burden' on industry or its labour costs, though there will be re-distribution *towards* those enterprises and services that are development orientated. The process of allocation of supporting finance for research (as for training) can build on existing mechanisms and state agencies initially, but the planning and negotiation process would naturally need to involve a growing role for participative planning, and shared responsibility within the enterprise.

(c) Given public financial constraints, it is clear that a high proportion of the public funding of aid for additional UK industrial and commercial development, and for additional public service activities, will be *selective* (i.e.work within governmental and legislative guidelines and priorities; will seek the maximum effective contribution from the recipient organisation). These are precisely circumstances which can be designed to encourage, or indeed *require*, extensive bargaining and consultation *within* the enterprise concerned, as to the changes and developments concerned, their employment and productivity implications, associated changes in operation and job functions, etc. This is particularly important if the selective guidelines affecting access to state funding encourage or require a wider sharing and pooling of resources and responsibilities between organisations (as an example in post-16 education, or in consortia activity involving more than one local authority, or in pooling of research and training initiatives).

(d) One important possibility that should not be neglected is that of the state instituting a system of company 'Investment Funds'. Essentially, what this involves is turning some part of any system of investment allowances against corporate tax liabilities into a socially controllable investment fund at enterprise level. In the mid 1970s, the Treasury in alliance with the Bank of England successfully resisted a serious attempt — backed by the TUC — to develop such a system in the UK (it had worked effectively in Sweden). The most straightforward way to operate such a scheme is to require a substantial proportion of such a company investment fund to be deposited, at a low or zero interest rate, with the Bank of England (or a state investment bank) until its release for spending on UK investment projects is agreed with the relevant state planning agency. This system can best be introduced at a time when government is raising tax allowances to encourage more investment. It not only provides a strong financial reason for companies to put forward additional investment projects; it also can be used to avoid excessive peaks and troughs (which was why its introduction here was supported in the mid 1970s by the UK machine tool industry — to the dismay of the Treasury, who wanted to present the idea as a dangerous left-wing heresy) and to give priority to particular locations or industrial sectors. It must be manifest that such a system could be effectively related to the functions of enterprise Participation Agreements.

(e) A reforming government *must* take steps to monitor and make more accountable major concentrations of monopoly and market power in the large companies; not least, as these, for a time at least, will include privatised public utilities with very considerable natural monopoly power.* Here we may emphasise the priority that will need to be given (i) to a strong and investigatory Price Commission, particularly *vis-a-vis* sectors with high levels of monopoly concentration or weak price competition (for example breweries, building materials) and (ii) to a much more principled and forward-looking scrutiny and control of take-overs. In the latter case it is important to go beyond narrow competition-based issues to a positive concern for the maintenance not only of current activities but also of development and investment effort in the UK, and a major emphasis on strengthening research and technology in the UK enterprises concerned. The contemporary experience is that we confront not only manipulation of asset stripping, and short run

---

*These issues were dealt with in my article: 'The Dole Economy. Can We Plan Our Way Out?' in *Joint Action for Jobs*, ed.Ken Coates, Spokesman, Nottingham, 1986.

profit taking without a sound development strategy, but that we could be witnessing further massive retreats from an adequate UK industrial base in the name of 'rationalisation' and re-grouping of companies. Quite clearly all of such concerns are of deep and direct interest to UK trade unionists. Clearly, too, it must be a priority to develop new systems of accountability and state intervention which would expect to draw directly upon properly informed views and responses from organised labour in the companies involved (and their major competitors). These policy matters are *unavoidable* if a future government is going to tackle the major structural problems of our economy, and not least those practices that are blocking possible development and pursuing short run and speculative profits and asset sales over the recumbent bodies of displaced workers. The total and deeply irrational neglect of social costs in the accountancy cannot be tolerated, cannot be allowed to continue. On this the interests of organised labour and a reforming government should be at one.

(f) This line of argument needs to be taken a step further. There must be barriers to large scale redundancies and closures, while proper economic and social audits examine the *real* costs and benefits involved and the constructive alternatives that could be pursued (under changed ownership if need be). That process must come close to the agencies of industrial democracy. Positively, the time has come to put a public obligation on all major enterprises to submit annually a review of their UK employment creation projects in the previous period, and proposals for new employment creation in the forthcoming period. Such an obligation could be aided by a far more flexible deployment of taxes/allowances on employment and particularly on newly generated employment. (For example, cutting employers' National Insurance payments by 1% of payroll is a very blunt instrument, doing much more to create an indiscriminate increase in profitability than to generate jobs. But a proportionately large reduction, say 10 per cent of payroll for two years on jobs created through new investment projects might have more employment effect for less cost to the Exchequer). While on this subject, it should be said that the present system of employment taxes is indefensible; for one thing it is more and more encouraging avoidance of tax by organising employment and earnings below the NI threshold, and by dismissing regular workers and employing others on labour sub-contracts. We need a payroll tax supplemented by surcharges related to the use of labour-only sub-contracts to wipe out the main areas of tax dodging. Now, all these matters are once again of direct concern to organised labour. And again, the programme and approach we need is one which establishes the new emphasis by the state on responsible employment policies *in alliance* with organised labour that has been given the opportunity to work away on the same problems *within the enterprise* and with effective rights and resources to do so.

(To be more challenging, given the sheer scale of unemployment, we should be setting limits to annual contracted hours of work for full-time staff, and limits to actual annual hours of work too. These might work on a two-tier basis, with absolute prohibition over a given level, and employment tax surcharge over a lower level — with a phased programme to reduce such levels over time. That in itself would force employers and unions to re-examine work organisation and practices, and recruitment and training requirements.)

It would have been perfectly possible to have extended the listing of state measures of planning/accountability beyond the ones put forward above. But enough has been said to make clear the crucial argument. That is, we can and should generate through a crucial series of essential planning and development measures a whole new range of functions to be handled urgently by organised labour through enterprise-wide systems of bargaining and wider participation in know-how and decision-making and its implementation. Abstracting a category of revised 'labour law' to be thought of at arms length from such challenging economic processes could mean we miss important opportunities of extending trade union function and real democratisation. Let me take one subject area, deliberately left out of the above listing, which might help to clinch the argument. For over 10 years now we have had one clear and straightforward example of a subject area where state initiative and regulation has directly reinforced and extended trade union functions and collective rights; that area has been health and safety. It was a useful Trojan Horse for industrial democracy, and not strongly resisted because of widespread public recognition that the social costs and benefits involved should not be suppressed. That matter felt like an adjunct to labour law and to an existing range of protective legislation. We have to make all the other topics that have been listed seem as constructively relevant. Meanwhile, we should be picking up the 'old' familiar subject of health and safety and pushing out its frontier once again; conceptually we are struggling for an advancing 'frontier of control' here as elsewhere. The way to do it is to put on the industrial agenda, the agenda and institutions of *joint* health and safety work, the wider question of possible sources of danger and pollution to the environment from the operation of the enterprise — the external costs that may be neglected and inflicted on local communities. The TUC is rightly speaking up strongly on UK responsibilities for acid rain. Our industrial democracy has to reach out to these wider responsibilities.

Finally, to a topic that requires a separate paper but cannot be left out of the discussion: *Pension Funds*. the same principles apply. What is needed is *both* a development of legislation that gives a firm basis of rights to fund members and their representatives at enterprise level, *and* a new programme which relates the tax position of such funds to a new statement of their economic and social responsibilities. On the question of rights, we need not only a firm basis for putting all the key decision-making work of pension funds on to a joint basis (possibly with more provision to use arbitration if differences are entrenched). We also need a redefinition in law that makes clear the funds constitute *deferred pay*, and a redefinition of trustee responsibilities *and* of the responsibilities of financial advisers and managers. (It would make sense also to provide that a modest proportion of the flow of funds could be used to provide relative collective services for scheme members; this should include access to impartial and expert financial advice, and bargained concessions on a wide range of expenditures). The state in particular should be requiring accountability not only to members, but in terms of reports as to the contribution to UK development and employment made by the allocation of funds. The highly privileged position of such funds needs to be linked directly to investment flows in the UK, and should not be extended to excessive levels of financial investment outside the UK. There should be more specific encouragement to those funds that have developed an active role, in financial and managerial terms, in UK based development capital. The emphasis of any redefinition of trustee (and adviser) responsibility should be on asset holding and management that should offer *long term* returns to match long term obligations, that should respect the need for adequate development and employment creation in the UK (without which the employment base itself can only erode). Given that the real rate of return on financial investment is high, and has been for some years now, there is no contradiction between a UK investment bias and the ensuring of positive returns for members.

Chapter 7

Women, Fair Wages and Employment Rights

Emma MacLennan

Introduction

The European Social Charter states that it is one of the "fundamental social and economic rights" of all workers to receive "fair remuneration such as will give them and their families a decent standard of living" (Article 4). Britain is a signatory to that Charter, yet in 1985 more than half of all women in full-time work (52.7 per cent) and over three-quarters of all women working part-time (79.2 per cent) received less than the 'decency threshold' for earnings specified in the Charter (in 1985-86, £115 per week or £2.90 per hour). Women form over two-thirds of all low paid workers in Britain, and nearly six million women are low paid — over a quarter of the entire adult workforce. Since 1979 the problem has increased: then two-thirds of all full-time manual women workers were low paid, while today the proportion has risen to three-quarters.

In recent years the increase in women's employment, their growing participation in trade unions, and the anger of women themselves, have pushed the issue of women's pay higher in the political agenda. Fair pay and fair treatment for women workers have been at the heart of the debate surrounding low pay and the comparative effectiveness of trade union action or minimum wage legislation.

This chapter will examine the position of women workers in the labour market in the mid 1980s, and consider the role of legislation in determining women's pay and status in employment. The present Conservative Government's policy of deregulation and weakening of employment protections has had a profound effect on women's employment, and will continue to undermine the efforts of women and their trade unions to gain equal treatment and fair pay for women workers. Legal rights which underpin those efforts are therefore essential if improvements in women's employment status are to be achieved with the urgency that women demand.

Trends in Women's Employment

The greatest changes in labour market activity during the 1970s and '80s have related to women's employment, and in particular the employment of married women. In 1971 women formed 36 per cent of all employees in Britain, compared to 44.7 per cent in 1986. Much of this increase can be accounted for by the boom in part-time working, especially in recent years. Since 1983, the entire growth in women's employment has been due to a rise in the number of part-time workers.

At the same time that women's labour market participation has grown, women's earnings have increased relative to those of men. Women's gross weekly and hourly earnings improved in relative terms by some 15 per cent in the 1970s, although achieving a peak in 1976-77. Moreover, this increase represented a real improvement which cannot otherwise be explained by changes in the industrial, occupational or age distributions of men and women in employment, or by changes in hours worked[1].

A further major growth area for women during this period has been their representation in trade unions. Since the early 1970s, the total number of female trade union members has risen by close to one-third, so that now some 30 per cent of all union members are women. Moreover, particularly in the early 1970s, the growth in actual union membership among women has outstripped the growth in women's employment, so that the density of women's trade union membership has increased[2]. This growth has occurred most markedly in the public sector.

But while recent years have seen a growth in women's employment, union organization, and relative earnings, in other respects their position in the labour market has improved little and may now be deteriorating.

'Secondary' Workers

The increase in the number of women workers in the 1970s and '80s has occurred almost entirely in sectors already dominated by female employment. In 1979 the distributive trades and service industries together employed nearly two-thirds of the female working population — 63.3 per cent in all. By 1985 this proportion had increased to over three-quarters.

Women's employment has also become more firmly fixed in the 'secondary' labour market of poorly paid work with little job security. In the 1980s, with rising unemployment among full-time male and female workers, the number of casual, seasonal, and temporary jobs — mainly done by women — has grown. By one estimate, about seven per cent of the workforce now consists of temporary workers[3].

The 'casualisation' of women's employment is partly accounted for by the growth in the services sector as a source of jobs, in which part-time and seasonal work has always been prominent. But there has been a declining inclination amongst employers throughout industry to take on permanent full-time staff. This inclination has been encouraged by the comparative lack of employment protection given to part-time and temporary workers. In the 1980s, the Government's policy of deregulation has considerably reduced the protection offered to many women in employment, and has consequently worsened their conditions of work.

Women and Deregulation

The improvement of women's position in the labour market has no more than a token role to play in current government policy. Even the Equal Pay Act of 1970 has been decried by government ministers for preventing "employers from restricting pay to what is necessary to secure employees"[4].

The aim of employment policy since 1979 has been to dismantle restrictions on the free working of the labour market as far as possible. High unemployment has been tolerated by a Government intent on reducing wages and the bargaining power of labour. In turn they blame unemployment on working people, whom the Government argue have 'priced themselves' and others 'out of the market'. Their solution is lower pay and the transformation of the British economy into one of 'low tech or no tech' jobs.

Women in particular have suffered from this passion for deregulation, beginning with the Employment Act in 1980. This was introduced by the Government in order to restrict the rights of trade unions to organise and act on behalf of their members, and also to address what were described as 'burdens and barriers to business'. Many of these 'burdens' were rights which had been established as recently as the 1976 Employment Protection Act, which had provided legal minimum standards to underpin negotiated agreements and what was recognised as good employment practice.

The 1980 Employment Act increased the length of service required in order to qualify for unfair dismissal from six months to one year for all full-time workers, while in small firms (employing no more than 20 staff) the period was extended to two years. Maternity protections, already subject to a two-year qualification, were also weakened by the Act. All firms employing fewer than six members of staff were no longer required to reinstate female employees after maternity leave. For eligible women, the procedure necessary to qualify for reinstatement was made more complex and inaccessible.

Fair Wage Protections

The Employment Act also abolished Schedule 11 of the Employment Protection Act, which provided for the compulsory arbitration of wages. Schedule 11 gave legal backing to minimum negotiated standards of pay and conditions. In the years in which it operated, claims for fair pay under Schedule 11 had most benefited groups of workers on relatively low rates of pay — a provision which stood in the way of the Conservative Government's desire for wage cuts.

One by one other employment protections have been dismantled. The Fair Wages Resolution, established in 1891 as "the protector of the standards of competence and honour of industry as a whole", was abolished by Government regulation in 1983. Like Schedule 11, the Fair Wages Resolution provides for fair pay. Firms operating under government contracts were required to maintain standards of pay and conditions of work no less favourable than those applying to directly employed staff in the public sector. The abolition of the resolution opened the door to wage-cutting competition by private companies eager to win lucrative contracts in the public sector.

The Wages Act 1986 further reduced legal minimum wage protections. Its target was the wages councils — tripartite statutory bodies comprised of representatives of both sides of industry, along with three independent members, which since 1909 had set legal minimum rates of pay and conditions of work in the lowest paid industries. Britain's 27 wages councils covered some 2.7 million workers, three-quarters of whom were women. Moreover, wages council minimum rates of pay were of much greater significance to women's pay than to men in the same industries. On average the minimum rates accounted for 75-100 per cent of women's actual earnings, compared to 60-75 per cent of the earnings of men[5].

The Wages Act 1986 removed the protection of minimum

wages from young people aged under 21 who were employed in wages council industries. Some 500,000 young workers lost their right to a legal minimum rate of pay, two-thirds of whom were young women. Other wages council provisions — for example setting overtime rates and minimum holidays — were also abolished. In combination with cuts of over one-third in the number of wages inspectorate staff empowered to enforce the remaining provisions of the wages councils, women's rights to 'fair remuneration' were drastically reduced.

'Burdens on Business'

The Government's 1985 Trade and Industry White Paper *Burdens on Business*, plus reforms announced in the 1986 Budget Statement, and a 1986 Employment White Paper entitled *Building Business...Not Barriers* have together introduced a package of further deregulation which will significantly damage women's conditions of employment.

The qualification period to claim unfair dismissal has been raised to two years for all full-time workers. Because part-time workers already face a five-year qualification period, the Government propose to raise the hours of work thresholds which define part-time work for the purpose of employment rights, so that fewer will be eligible.

As a result of these 'technical' changes, 1.9 million part-time and 6.7 million workers in all will be ineligible to claim basic employment rights due to inadequate length of service qualifications. Over one-quarter of the entire workforce, the majority of them women, will be unprotected by unfair dismissal, maternity or redundancy rights. More than 2 in 5 female part-time workers will be exempt from such basic provisions as the right to an itemised pay slip.

In small firms, where women's employment is most concentrated, these exemptions will come on top of special allowances for small firm employers already given in employment legislation. For all basic employment rights, industrial tribunals are instructed to take into account the size of firm in determining a settlement or assessing the "reasonableness" of an employer's behaviour. Now firms employing fewer than 10 staff are to be exempt altogether from statutory maternity provisions.

In low-paying industries such as hotels and catering, where small firms predominate, some 30 per cent of all women employees will be unprotected by maternity rights due to this special allowance alone. Throughout industry as a whole, *at least* half a million women are employed in firms which will be exempt from maternity legislation due to their size[6].

Thus, by making employment rights dependent on length of service, by applying more stringent eligibility rules to part-time workers, and by giving special exemptions to small firms, the Government have successfully taken away from a large proportion of women workers any legal rights which underpin their security of employment. This lack of legal recourse has not pushed women into the arms of trade unions and collective action. Rather, it has made union organisation in the lowest paid industries more difficult.

Obstacles to Trade Union Organisation

In the private sector, the hotel and catering industry typifies women's low paid employment. More than two in every five men, and four out of every five women working in the industry., earn less than the Council of Europe's 'decency threshold' for pay. Half of the industry's workforce is part-time, and three-quarters are women. The majority of firms are small, often owner-managed businesses. Nine out of every ten hotel and catering firms have fewer than 20 staff, and over half of the workforce is employed in such small firms. The level of union organisation, particularly among the small firms, is extremely low: according to one estimate, just six per cent of the total hotel and catering workforce are in unions[7].

There are tremendous obstacles to union recruitment in these circumstances. In a small cafe or take-away restaurant employing only a handful of staff, the bargaining power of workers is weak. Statutory employment protections such as the right to claim unfair dismissal could be important in underpinning the strength of trade unions, but the most vulnerable workers (part-timers, casual workers, seasonal staff) fail to qualify.

Many are not prepared to confront their employers for fear of losing their jobs. Although sacking a worker for trade union activity is illegal whatever the length of service, appeals to industrial tribunals on these grounds are notoriously unsuccessful. On average only one in six cases are resolved in favour of the worker. Moreover, the complainants may be liable to pay their employer's costs if their case fails.

A further, practical obstacle to union recruitment is the sheer effort involved. In private services such as hotels or shops the resources and staff time which would be absorbed in obtaining members in hundreds of thousands of small workplaces pose real difficulties for the unions involved. Part-time workers in particular face difficulties in becoming involved in a union — for example, problems in attending meetings or obtaining information about union activities. In hotels and catering, where nationally labour turnover is around 70 per cent per year, new members may not remain in the union for long[8]. USDAW, the shopworkers' union, reckon that they need to recruit one-third of their membership annually in order to maintain total numbers.

For these and other reasons union membership among women working in these industries, in present circumstances, is likely to remain very low.

The Public Sector
The public sector also employs vast numbers of low paid women workers. Nearly one and a quarter million workers in Britain, over five per cent of the entire workforce, are employed as local authority manual workers or as ancilliaries in the National Health Service. Some three-quarters of local authority manuals and 70 per cent of ancilliaries are women, most of whom work part-time. Virtually all of these workers are low paid.

Partly because of the numbers of workers employed in these jobs, the Government is intent on cutting public sector wages (and their cost to the Exchequer) at the bottom end of the pay scale. The Government's policy of privatisation and contracting out work in public services has been explicitly aimed at undermining the position of public sector unions, and particularly union rates of pay and conditions of work.

Many low paid women working in the school meals service, as hospital cleaners, in laundries, or in staff canteens, have had their jobs put out to tender to private firms. With the rescission of the Fair Wages Resolution, legal rules for competitive tendering, and the heat of competition for public contracts, wage cuts have been the rule for workers in these sectors. One employers' organisation, the Contract Cleaning and Maintenance Association, estimated that rates of pay have been cut by an average of 20 per cent (*Financial Times*, November 1984).

Equal Pay
The 1970 Equal Pay Act provided for equal pay for men and women employed by the same firm and engaged in the same or broadly similar work. In addition to this, pay structures and collective agreements were also to be non-discriminatory. It undeniably made an impact on the relative pay of women — as we have seen, women's relative earnings rose by 15 per cent

during the 1970s, most of which can be attributed to legislative intervention. But due to weakness in the legislation itself, this improvement seems to have been a 'one-off' effect, and women's relative position is stabilising at around three-quarters of male earnings.

The Equal Pay Act improved women's pay by forcing employers to integrate recognised pay scales in a number of industries, and to remove the most glaring inequities. But the effectiveness of the legislation has been limited by job segregation, which makes it impossible for women to compare their wages with men engaged in the same work. Moreover, in jobs such as typing or nursing, the few men who are employed tend to be as lowly paid as their female colleagues. For these reasons, being able to claim "equal pay for work of equal value" is an important improvement in the effectivenenss of the legislation. For the same reasons any such amendment to the Equal Pay Act has been strongly resisted by the Government.

European Community directives calling for rights to claim equal pay for equal value have forced the Government to introduce amending legislation, which they have grudgingly done. The European Court ruled that the Equal Pay Act had failed to comply with the EC Directive on Equal Treatment, as claims for equal value could only be taken where an employer had agreed to the use of a job evaluation scheme. In 1984 new rules widened the scope for equal value by allowing claims without the need for an existing job evaluation scheme.

As a result, according to the Annual Report of the 1986 TUC's Women's Conference, claims for equal value have increased markedly since 1984. Claims of up to 28 per cent are now being won by women in a wide range of occupations. Major equal value claims have been launched by a number of unions on behalf of their women members — including the Transport Workers (TGWU), the General and Municipal (GMBATU), the Banking Union (BIFU), the Scientific and Technical Union (ASTMS), the Mineworkers (NUM), and many others. The clerical union Apex, for example, had 24 equal value claims before industrial tribunals in one month in 1986, with another 114 in preparation[9].

Successful claims have been pursued despite some shortcomings in the new rules. Even if a woman succeeds in establishing equal value with her male comparator, an employer may continue to pay different rates of pay if there is a "genuine material factor" (including the effect of market forces) which justifies continued differentials. The procedures for taking a claim are complex and lengthy. There have also been some setbacks — such as the case of the cook at Cammell Laird who was granted equal value with skilled shipyard workers, but has been told by a recent industrial tribunal that she would not get equal pay because of differences in her holiday entitlement and other conditions of employment.

But the success of many other equal value claims has shown the way in which legislation can underpin the efforts of trade unions to improve the position of their members, particularly those who have less 'industrial muscle' to employ. The growth in equal value claims will have far-reaching implications for the position and status of women throughout industry. As the experience of equal value illustrates, the limitations of existing legislation should not be a reason for rejecting the potential role of law as a tool for winning improvements for working people — a tool which can be put to best use by workers collectively through their unions.

Employment Rights and Fair Pay

A solution to the problem of women's low pay cannot be found solely through a reliance on collective bargaining. In low-paying industries where union organisation is weak — particularly among women working in small firms, in part-time jobs, as homeworkers, or temporary staff — major gains in union organisation will not occur without better legal rights to job security. In the public sector, little headway can be made so long as private contractors are allowed free rein to undercut union rates of pay and conditions of work.

The importance of employment protection in helping unions to achieve improvements for their lowest paid members is reinforced by the Thatcher Government's anxiety to dismantle employment protection legislation in order to cut wages and "price workers into jobs". The growing problem of low pay has not held back the swell of record levels of unemployment. But it has weakened the strength of trade unions in low paid sectors and has increased divisions in the labour market, with a wider pool of 'casual' workers with little or no employment rights.

Fair pay for women workers requires fair employment protection — rights which underpin, not undermine, union organisation. A package of individual rights is needed which includes better protection against victimisation at work and dismissal, better job security for pregnant women and better treatment for women returning to work after maternity leave. For women working in part-time jobs or as homeworkers, rights to information, access to trade unions and measures to enable them to attend and participate in union meetings are essential if they themselves are to make their views heard through their unions. For women working in the most casual and exploitative circumstances, better legal rights to documentation — such as itemised payslips, comprehensive written contracts, and published payscales — would make a tangible difference to their ability to fight back against their pay and conditions.

Legal rights to fair pay and a national statutory minimum wage would do much to improve the position of women workers. As with the equal value provisions of the equal pay legislation, these rights could become an important instrument used primarily by trade unions to obtain improvements for their women members.

The Labour Party-TUC Liaison Committee has in 1986 produced a joint statement which recognises the inadequacy of collective bargaining alone to deal with low pay. It points to the importance of statutory support such as the wages councils, fair wages provisions, and rights to equal pay. It also outlines a strategy for the introduction of a national minimum wage for all workers, backed by law and enforced mainly through collective bargaining.

The national minimum wage would be expressed as an hourly minimum, covering part-time workers, homeworkers, casual employees, and anyone in work on an equal basis. Initially this minimum would be agreed in consultation with trade unions collectively — submissions to the TUC in response to their discussion paper on minimum wages suggest a starting figure equivalent to £80 for a full-time week.

The minimum wage legislation would include provision for uprating this figure to a higher target level, while the speed of phasing would be dependent upon negotiation between the unions and a Labour Government. Alternatively, legislation could provide for a fixed period of phasing towards an agreed target. Contrary to fears that this would be tantamount to incomes policy, a fixed period of phasing would give more certainty to the low paid, and allow less scope for government intervention.

Where an employer fails to observe the minimum wage, unions will be able to enforce the minimum by making group claims to the Central Arbitration Committee (CAC), which will be empowered to make a binding award. Unions will be able to pursue claims in workplaces where they may only have one member, and the minimum wage will then become a contractual right for all employees in the firm. Where there are no union members present, individual complaints will be referred to a new Minimum Wages Inspectorate, which will also be able to prosecute in cases of persistent underpayment.

Because most referals to the CAC will be by trade unions on behalf of their low paid female members, enforcement of the minimum wage will be similar to the experience of equal value claims. Fair differentials — based on skill, responsibility, and compensation for risk — will not be threatened.

Minimum wage legislation, of course, will not be sufficient in itself to end the problem of women's low pay. But as part of a package of employment protections to build job security and encourage union membership, legal rights to minimum wages can do much to improve the position of women workers in employment. A legal floor to wages which reflects the unions' belief that no one should earn less than an acceptable level of pay would do much to ensure fairer pay for all low paid workers.

References

1. Chiplin *et al*, "Relative Female Earnings in Great Britain and the Impact of Legislation" in *Women and Low Pay*, ed. P. Sloane, MacMillan, London, 1980.
2. Bain and Price, "Union Growth: Dimemsions, Determinants and Destiny", in *Industrial Relations in Britain*, ed. G. Bain, Basil Blackwell, Oxford, 1983.
3. *Financial Times*, 6.1.86.
4. Sir Geoffrey Howe, *Daily Mirror*, 25.5.83.
5. See *Who Needs the Wages Councils*, Low Pay Unit pamphlet No. 24, 1983.
6. Estimate based on *Business Monitor Size Analysis*, 1985.
7. See *Waiting for Change*, ed. D. Byrne, Low Pay Unit pamphlet No. 42, 1986.
8. *Ibid*.
9. *Financial Times*, 10.3.86.

III
Trade Union Action
for
Freedom and Fairness

Without an adequate legal framework, unions will not be able to operate freely. But to regain the social initiative they must do far more than simply regain their former legal status. To recover power, unions need to create a new internationalism, capable of responding to transnational economic power. They need to acquire a capacity to initiate actions, and shape a future, rather than simply responding to attacks, and defending the past.

Chapter 8

Uniting the Fragments
John Edmonds

It would be hard to imagine a more challenging and uncertain future than that which the trade unions now face. Yet in a *Back to the Future* way (or is it Forward to the Past?) we are still occupied in trying to find answers to the problems of the 1970s.

We are still in the world of a senior steward in a large manufacturing plant, where the concerns of male, manual and middle-aged members outshine all others. Skill differentials remain the most pressing issue. Industrial democracy is simply a matter of adapting and extending industrial relations procedures that are already formalised and relatively advanced.

Millions of workers live in an entirely different world. For them, the real concern is getting off first base: winning the right to trade union membership, raising poverty wages, avoiding discrimination or victimisation, dealing with arbitrary and aggressive management.

Please don't misunderstand my argument — I am not saying "forget male manufacturing workers or industrial democracy." Throughout large areas of industry, trade union membership has survived remarkably well and has pretty consistently delivered benefits to the workers. But industrial, demographic and technical trends point to a shrinking of these well-organised sectors and the growth of a new class of exploited workers. Consider these trends. Between 1980 and 1985, more than 1.4 million jobs in manufacturing were lost and another half million will disappear by 1990. New jobs are being created only in private services, and these jobs are primarily for part-time women workers; nearly all the new employment (95 per cent) recorded since 1983 has been for female part-timers. Tied to these changes, full-time jobs will fall by over a million between 1984 and 1990, whereas part-time jobs are set to rise by 900,000; and male employment will drop by 600,000 as against a rise in female employment of 400,000. The shift in work is also away from the heartlands of the labour movement to areas with less of a tradition in trade unionism.

These are fundamental changes. Millions of exploited workers — overwhelmingly women working part-time in service industries or service occupations in other industries — are being removed from trade union protection. Their legal rights are feeble and frequently non-existent. The degree of collective organization is weak.

It is in this sphere, too, that the politics of Thatcherism have been at their most consistent and integrated. The contracting-out of work from the public services; the scrapping of Fair Wages protection; the whittling away of employment and maternity rights; the dismantling of the health and safety apparatus: all these link together in the push for deregulation and 'flexibility'. It is a strategy as much about imposing acquiescence and closing down opportunities as about cutting employment costs. At its heart is a very clear picture of the kind of employment which should be on offer in the future. It is a picture of a *servant* economy more than a service economy.

Trade unionism can only meet this challenge if it recognises these realities. For a start we must accept that, for the vast majority of the workers on this new front line, trade unionism is distant, belongs to other types of workers, and is increasingly preoccupied with very inward and frankly incomprehensible wrangles. I cannot, for example, see much appeal to these workers in the 'market' or 'business' unionism promoted by some commentators and unions. This model seems geared only to a small part of the workforce (generally on a secure inside track). It also seems to be, in essence, a promotional policy for unions based on an appeal to employers and on 'delivering' a workforce to them as part of a package.

In my view, the trade unions should put themselves forward as champions of the new exploited workers. At the centre of their campaign should be a demand for a new systematic set of rights for people at work, which would rectify the appalling vulnerability of British workers to unfair and arbitrary treatment:

- A right to secure employment would cover unfair dismissal, periods of notice and redundancy.
- A right to a fair wage would guarantee minimum earnings, hours of work and holidays.
- A right to equal treatment would enforce equal pay for work of equal value — a measure of central importance for women at work — and would also gear employment-generating measures directly to the elimination of sex and race bias.
- A right to safe and healthy work would cover stress at work

and comfort as well as the control of hazards and dangers.

● A right to free association would deal in concrete terms — and from the worker's point of view — with the issues which too often are buried in the frankly boring discussion about whether trade unions as institutions should have immunities or positive rights. At stake here is the baseline right and ability of workers to group together without victimisation, to be able to call on representation and facilities and — on the rare occasions when it arises — to be able to withdraw their labour.

All these rights relate to workers as individuals and groups — albeit increasingly small and isolated groups. So the *second* central element of a new approach is about unions as the monitors and enforcers of such a system. If taken seriously this role would have enormous implications for unions and for union officers. The old model of a Negotiating Man's Union — dispensing from above policies, bargaining solutions and the maintenance of a well-oiled procedural machine — has to go. The priority will be bringing together isolated and fragmented groups, helping to enforce their rights and, most important, giving them for the first time the self-confidence to do it themselves.

As far as workplace issues are concerned, a new order of priorities is likely. Equal rights, health and safety, the working environment, and very basic concerns of pay, conditions and the way in which workers are treated by employers for whom 'industrial relations' is a meaningless phrase — all of these will rise to the surface.

But to emphasise the point: the challenge to trade unionism will not just be the issues which it takes up, but the way in which it takes them up. If the politics of Thatcherism is about isolating workers, narrowing their vision of the possible and cutting off their means of support, the response by trade unionism must tackle this politics head on. It must involve, it must foster self-supporting groups, it must put the means of widening opportunities back in workers' hands, it must, to use the jargon, *enable*.

This, in turn, means that trade unionism cannot be limited to the workplace — especially a workplace which has been so confined and impoverished. Unions must increasingly find a stronger place in the non-work areas of the lives of members and potential members. Trade unionism ought to be central to popular culture — to local group expression and participation, from sports to rock concerts. All too often we celebrate the past connection of unions with popular culture while the present ossifies.

Unions can and should provide benefits for members not only

as workers, but also as consumers, as holiday-makers, as parents, as motorists, and so on. Here again, however, the special contribution which trade unionism can make is to fight back against the individualising trends of Conservatism. There is massive scope for helping to build or re-create self-supporting communities and networks, based wherever possible on a pooling of information and advice and a genuinely collective provision and exchange.

All of this seems to me to represent something which is very far from a non-political trade unionism. If, beyond that, it is hard to classify such ideas into one camp or another, that just may be a sign of how far what passes for politics in trade unions has become impoverished and introspective.

Tailoring a response to the main points of attack of Thatcherism is not about the influence of union general secretaries. It is about following up the central message of the unions' political fund ballots: saying "Yes to a Voice", and giving a voice to more and more people who won't get it through any other means.

And, of course, that means also saying 'yes' to a voice within the union itself. More points of access and contact with and within unions will be crucial if such an approach is to be not just about image — but about a reality of self-confidence, security and influence on the part of those who are presently unorganised and exploited.

In the last few months there have been some genuine attempts in the trade unions to debate openly these central problems which we face. There have been false starts and there have been some very unhelpful diversions — notably the construction of models that owe more to the personalities (real or media-perceived) of particular general secretaries than to the priorities of working people.

Meanwhile, the growth of the new servant class of exploited workers presents trade unionism with a major challenge. Their attachment to trade unions is very weak, yet we often speak as though there was still an automatic and unproblematic identity of interest between trade unions — as institutions — and working people. If we are to rise to the challenges of changing patterns of work, we do need to acknowledge the remarkably low esteem into which unions have fallen.

This is not just a question of the public standing of trade union officials (although the fact that the Gallup index regularly finds that only estate agents are trusted less by the public really should be a cause for concern). It involves recognising that the traditional reasons for joining a union, which are essentially negative or defensive in their nature, won't wash. It is just no good telling a woman working as a cleaner or cook that she should join a union or otherwise she'll get lousy pay and conditions. Unions — let's face it — haven't been able to stop poverty pay and appalling conditions in these areas.

Nor, since they have not been able to prevent job losses and redundancies, can they base their appeal on an argument that unionism is all that stands between a worker and job insecurity.

My argument is that if we are really going to get a grip on the future we are going to have to face up to some disquieting truths about the changing economic and political shape of our society. At the moment, trade unions are in danger of finding themselves utterly irrelevant to the needs of workers in that changing society.

This chapter was first published in *New Socialist* (June, 1986).

Chapter 9

Redistribution — Three Key Dimensions

Stuart Holland

Conventional capitalist economic theory has tended to treat technical change as a residual factor. It has been consigned to the background of most reasoning on economic growth and distribution. This is reflected in the standard production function of most conventional argument, i.e. the Cobb-Douglas function which treats production as a function of capital and labour with other factors as residual.

Marx's analysis of the impact of technical change is far more insightful. His concept of the rising organic and technical composition of capital is integrated in an analysis of the dynamics of capital accumulation, its impact on labour and social distribution, and on the spatial distribution of economic activity.

In contemporary terms this could be represented as a three dimensional process in which structural change (vertical axis) has both social and spatial implications (other axes). The mechanics of the process work through the creation of a reserve army of labour through both push and pull effects, i.e. the displacement of labour in industry by technical progress and the attraction of labour from declining sectors (displaced from agriculture and attracted to industry).

In the period of postwar expansion industry typically attracted young people from agriculture who did not wish to follow their parents into farming, while the offspring of workers in industry frequently made social progress into services. Spatially this was paralleled by a move from country to town, or rural-urban migration.

This paper was prepared for the conference of Socialism in the World at Cavtat in Yugoslavia. These arguments are elaborated and extended in *The Political Economy*, which will be published by Weidenfeld and Nicolson in 1987.

For most of the post-war period this was accompanied by both capital widening and capital deepening. In other words, the expansion of investment by-and-large resulted in more jobs rather than less. Thus, less employment in a given industrial sector was offset by the creation of more jobs in industry overall.

The most marked phenomenon of the post-war period was the increase in public services employment. Overall, in most of the countries of the European Economic Community (EEC), public civilian employment increased from around a fifth or a quarter of total employment to around, or more than, a half. This was symptomatic of the period of welfare statism or consensus capitalism in the developed capitalist countries, based on economic growth and a combination of labour intensive and labour extensive economies.

However, the arguments on rising technical composition of capital stressed by Marx a century or more ago have now been registered with devastating effect. In his own time Marx observed this process but underestimated the extent to which the rise of entirely new industries in chemicals and their derivatives, electrical engineering and petroleum based sectors (including the motor car) would create employment which would offset the decline of jobs in other sectors.

Between the wars, many of the products which had previously been 'upper-class' (such as cars) became middle-class consumption goods. After the Second World War, many of the middle-class goods, such as refrigerators and washing machines as well as cars, became working-class goods. This was apart from a new stimulus to job creation from the technical revolution in electrical engineering, jet aircraft, pharmaceuticals and nuclear power.

However, from the later 1960s it was increasingly evident that the rate of growth of employment in modern industry was falling off relative to the reconstruction years of the 1950s. Traditional industry such as textiles, food, drink and tobacco, woodwork and non-metallic minerals showed high growth in the centrally-planned economies from 1960 to 1975, but virtually no job growth in North America and Europe. Only metal and chemical products showed employment growth on a significant scale (more than one per cent a year) in North American and European modern industry in the same period, and this was down to 2.5 per cent a year from 3.5 per cent a year in the 1950s.

Meanwhile, in West Germany, one of the strongest accumulators of capital in the 1950s, the rate of gross domestic fixed capital formation fell dramatically before the Organization of Petroleum Exporting Countries (OPEC) oil price rises — from 9 per cent a year between 1950-54, to 6 per cent between 1960-64, and only 0.2 per cent between 1970-74. In other words, even if the capital-labour ratios of the 1950s had been maintained, the rate of job creation would have fallen. By not renewing the work permits of immigrant workers from Yugoslavia, Greece and Turkey between 1974 and 1977, West Germany exported some two-thirds of a million guest workers and thus what would have been the highest registered level of unemployment of virtually any Organization for Economic Co-operation and Development (OECD) country in the 1970s.

There is no doubt that the deflationary monetarist policies of the leading capitalist countries are primarily responsible for the scale of the current unemployment in OECD countries. But there is no 'normal' full-employment level to which to return, for the following reasons.

Evidence available from the new generation of mini-computers based on the silicone chip indicates that these are mainly labour displacing rather than job creating. They of course include robotics in industry and word and data processing in services.

It has been forecast by the Manpower Services Commission in Britain, by Nora and Minc in France, and by the Siemens Company in West Germany that between 30 per cent and 40 per cent of services employment in typing, data processing, clerical, design and related staff could be displaced by these technologies within the next 10 to 15 years. Individual studies of the application of these technologies in Britain confirm the forecasts at a micro level. This would be a devastating contraction of employment overall, granted that it has mainly been public and private services which hitherto in the post-war period have absorbed those workers displaced by technical progress in industry.

In industry the progress of robotics has been remarkable in the late 1970s in such countries as Japan , and is likely to be similar in Europe and the United States in the 1980s. A report prepared in 1978 by the Central Policy Review Staff of the British Government predicted that within 30 years Britain could produce all her projected material needs with only 10 per cent of the existing labour force in industry if robotics were extensively applied. In other words, the report projected 90 per cent technological unemployment. This report, prepared by Professor Stonier of the University of Bradford, has been criticized on various grounds. Trade union opposition, management inertia and other factors could well offset it. But its scale is nonetheless striking.

Some of the reaction to such forecasts is simply ostrich-like, claiming that such displacement of labour has never occurred before. But in fact it has occurred, throughout Europe and the United States, in the key sector of agriculture. From being the dominant employment sector in Britain, employment in agriculture by the turn of the last century was down to less than 15 per cent. In the EEC countries, agricultural employment was still as high as 25 per cent in the 1950s, but now is less than 10 per cent. In Britain agriculture now accounts for only 2.5 per cent of total labour, and in the United States only slightly more.

What appears to be happening throughout the developed capitalist countries is a process of innovation in techniques of production and processes themselves rather than product innovation. While it is possible that the new products such as mini-computers and data processors may create new employment opportunities on a significant scale, it also seems highly unlikely that they will create significant net employment. Major technological unemployment now appears more clearly on the agenda than when Marx wrote of rising technical and organic composition of capital in the 1860s.

Another irony or contradiction lies in the fact that if the governments of OECD succeed in one of their stated main objectives today, i.e. that of raising investment, they thereby also will raise unemployment in a manner more severe than anything witnessed in economic history.

Such factors indicate that there is no simple solution to the crisis of contemporary capitalism. The crisis is in substantial part due to the 'beggar-my-neighbour' policies of deflation imposed by monetarist governments who are seeking to re-structure capital through depressing wage costs. But a simplistic view of the current crisis not only fails to recognise that reducing wages reduces demand and thus sales and profits, but also fails to take account of the major redistribution of resources which would be necessary to achieve a recovery of either output or employment on a significant scale.

The diagram (see p.142) indicates the scale of the crisis and problems. It stresses the extent to which the structural crisis of technological unemployment simultaneously takes the form of a social crisis, with major spatial implications (i.e. implications for cities, regions and areas).

Translating the previous argument into the terms of the diagram, it is clear that a major contraction of both industry and services employment will have a specific social distribution. In Britain it is conventional to distinguish five social classes in the accounting of social statistics. The indications from available evidence on the impact of the current new technologies shows that these will include certain work categories normally identified

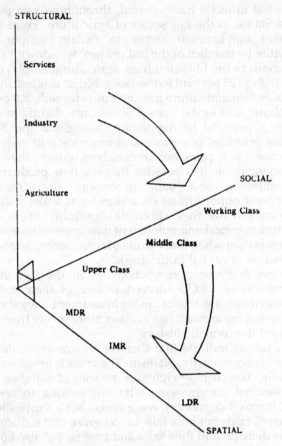

with management, i.e. draughtsmen, designers, technicians and those categories of management who in practice are occupied in routine administration. But the main impact of the technologies will be on the lower skilled, semi-skilled and unskilled workers in both industry and services, i.e. those categories four and five in British terms which constitute the main part of the working class.

Translating this again through to the spatial dimension of the diagram, it is evident that the impact of technical progress will not be spatially neutral. Distinguishing more developed regions (MDRs) from intermediate regions (IMRs) and less developed regions (LDRs), already available evidence indicates that the main effect of technical progress in relatively labour intensive industry is to displace labour in those areas and regions which were part of the 19th century industrial revolution, i.e. those which already are less developed. Intermediate regions in metal manufacture and engineering are especially prone to impact from robotics.

The categories adopted to describe regional distribution are relative. Thus they should not be conceived in a literal geographical sense. An intermediate or less developed area by current standards may well be an inner city area in a major metropolitan region. This certainly is the case with inner London, where there are today more unemployed than in a classic 'problem' region such as Wales, and where the outmigration of capital, combined with technical progress, has resulted in the loss of more than half a million jobs in manufacturing over more than 10 years.

The prospect of grave social tensions occurring because of the job loss and its spatial distribution from technical progress should not be underestimated. But the Northern Ireland case is instructive. In this region of the UK economy, average unemployment for a quarter century after the Second World War was double that of the rest of the United Kingdom, while unemployment among Catholics ranged to double or more that of Protestant workers. In inner London or inner Liverpool, youth unemployment can be double the national average (during a period in Britain when youth unemployment now is higher than at any time in the 1930s). Meanwhile, youth unemployment among ethnic minorities, such as those in the black community, typically is up to double that for youth unemployment as a whole.

Myths grow on such an unemployment. Attention tends to be focused on religion or race, rather than on the structural causes of the unemployment and its social and spatial impact. A bias arises against public programmes to alleviate unemployment, even when these are marginal or cosmetic. Overall, the bias against public spending and public works programmes is reflected in the political support for monetarist policies, with their assumption that public spending drains private spending and private initiative.

But in reality, in the unequally mixed economies of Western Europe and the United States, public spending sustains rather than drains the private sector. For instance, in Western Europe as a whole public enterprise typically represents less than 15 per cent of gross domestic product (GDP). This means that for any injection of 100 units of public spending, 85 units (whether £s sterling, francs, lire or marks) are spent in and generate income in the private sector. The relative recent failure of public spending to sustain full employment was less related to its income generating effects than the effects of structural change through technical progress in the developed economies, and its social and spatial distribution.

The contradiction is especially clear in the area of housing policy. In England and Wales more than 90 per cent of the public housing built is constructed by private enterprise firms. Therefore more than £90 of every £100 public spending cuts by the government in the nominally public sphere of council housing in practice is cut away from the private sector of construction. Meanwhile that sector is pouring hundreds of millions of pounds into speculative office development in projects which will mature during the 1980s in a period when the impact of micro-technologies such as data and word processors will reduce the demand for office staff and with it the demand for office space.

Therefore, a socialist policy aiming to counter the effects of new technologies on the structure of employment and its socio-spatial distribution cannot in any way neglect the primary importance of public spending. On the other hand, it also must take account of the structural, social and spatial distribution implications of the current trend in technical progress. In an era in which investment overall tends to displace rather than create jobs, a policy of (i) reflation must also take account of (ii) re-structuring, (iii) its social distribution and (iv) its spatial location of income and employment.

On a socialist basis there is a clear case for social redistribution *per se*, i.e. a shift of wealth from the upper class and a redistribution of income between the middle and working classes. But, again, the available information on the impact of technical progress indicates that such classic redistribution now also will need to be accompanied on a major scale by redistribution between sectors of activity and cities and regions. Social distribution of income itself is related to employment, even in a society of sizeable benefits and social security. Such redistribution, if serious, cannot neglect structural and spatial effects. Life opportunities in a real sense are frequently related not only to social class but also to the region or area in which one is born, and the available local employment.

In a clear sense this makes a socialist response to the current crisis more than ever relevant. Only policies for major redistribution are likely to offset or resolve the structural, social and spatial implications of technological change in the coming decades. In reality this makes imperative policies for not only (i) public spending on an unprecedented scale but also (ii) economic and social planning, and (iii) a new public sector including not only nationalised industry and services of the traditional model, but also new regional, municipal and local enterprise in the public sector (whether directly owned by the state authority or by workers' co-operatives). It also means a social negotiation of such major change in the economy and society, including shorter working time for those higher personal or social incomes made possible by the increased productivity from major technical progress.

In some firms, industries and services this will mean a 35 hour week. In others it may mean a 35 week year such as that enjoyed by many academics in higher education institutions. If such a concept of a standard 'sabbatical' for working people cannot be achieved, then social redistribution itself will not be basic and structural within the system. Further, such change can only be achieved in democratic fashion if it is with, rather than against, the workforce. But in reality this means not only industrial democracy at the place of work, but also an economic democracy extending to the wider issues of the distribution of resources between and within sectors, social groups and classes, and different areas and regions.

Such economic democracy implies that the planning necessary to adjust to the impact of technical progress cannot be from the 'top down', imposed in a technocratic manner by elites. Such elites may forecast the impact of technical change but cannot anticipate either the full range of social needs or the social resistance to specific forms of change. On the other hand, such economic democracy cannot either be simply from the 'bottom up'. There is no way in which workers in an individual factory or company can themselves independently gain an overview of the impact of technical change on the whole economy and society.

Thus, the interrelationships and inter-dependencies of structural, social and spatial dimensions to change must themselves be a multi-dimensional process in a new form of economic planning. Forecasts must be made on the best possible evidence of overall distribution of the effects of technical progress. But the inputs for such forecasting at the top or centre of the system must themselves come from the base. Moreover, the base cannot simply be the place of work, but must also include those either unemployed or about to become unemployed in the near future through the impact of technical change, as well as the elderly and retired.

This social dimension to redistribution also needs to be matched by the spatial dimension if the economics of regional deprivation is not to be complemented by the politics of protest, mystification and violence. The expansion of investment and those few jobs about to be created cannot simply occur in the more developed regions and areas of the system if the social and political cohesion of the system as a whole is to be maintained. There are many mechanisms for the representation of such interests, of which direct regional representation is only one. Crucially, there must be a link between the regional level and what is occurring at the national level in terms of the social and regional distribution of resources.

Above all, the economic planning involved in seeking to adapt to the consequences of technical progress must itself be a process rather than an administrative fiat or act. If the aim of economic progress is itself social progress and the development of the individual within the whole, then economic planning must itself increasingly become a process of social negotiation of changed options for the economy and with it for society as a whole. Which in turn implies a concept of social control. Such control in a democratic and socialist society implies control not over planning in the abstract but also over its distribution between firms and sectors, social groups and classes, and regions and areas.

Chapter 10

Democracy is the Essence
Stephen Bodington

Industrial democracy has too long been seen as a sort of amenity of Labour politics. Every citizen has a say in choosing governments: is it not only fair that every worker should have a say about the management of their work; involvement would reduce alienation, make work more pleasant — and so forth. Such sentiments are of course well founded but trivial. Democratic control over economic processes is the essence of socialist economics. Even now socialist movements are only half awake to this crucial perception and it has taken generations of bitter experience and laborious theorization and much turning back from dead ends to begin to glimpse a truth which — like many truths — once seen is simplicity itself.

Economic pragmatism is a valuable asset with which the British labour movement has always been richly endowed, but with this quality there has tended to go a certain coyness about theory. In fact, of course, there is no escaping from theory; generalisations, if not better then worse, inform all economic practice. So from time to time it is wise to have a look at theoretical concepts. British Labour whilst avoiding Marxist labels has in practice, like other socialist movements, adopted many Marxist concepts. The thoroughness of Marx's analysis opened many eyes to the nature of capitalism and, in particular, forms of capitalist exploitation. Armed with this understanding movements saw, as an immediate objective, the winning back of surplus value which capitalism was taking from them. But Marx's — or anyone else's — analysis, of what is, only most vaguely and indirectly throws light on what might be instead.

Circumstances today shout loud to us that the old game of winning for ourselves a bigger share of the values produced by capital is fast running out of steam. For this reason serious and accurate thought about profoundly different economic alternatives suddenly becomes of immediate practical importance. And that is why we have to ask in a very practical way "Alternatives to what?" Just to say "Alternatives to capitalism" is not of much practical use. We need to look at capitalist *practice* and know with what practice we should challenge it, what we should set against it, and also who is to do the setting of the new practice against the old.

Long ago, in the 1860s, a resolution of the International Workingmen's Association on Trades Unions spoke about the need for trade unions to become organising centres for superseding 'the Wages System' — an interesting way of expressing the need for an alternative, one that it is worth giving some thought to. To speak of the existing system as 'the wages system' has a practical ring to it in that much of the world's work gets done because people now sell their capabilities for wages to managements who decide how they are to be used. The ideas that dominate economic management in a capitalist society are money, cost and profit. These are practical ideas that guide everyday decisions. Economic decisions are motivated by hopes of selling products for more than their costs. Money facilitates buying; lack of money prevents it. To get money, people seek employment, that is sell a part of themselves for wages or salaries. This whole structure of buying and selling drives the system as it were automatically, through 'market forces'. The guidance of these concepts governs the day by day economic practice of millions of people.

If one studies the implications of economic practice governed by buying and selling one gets to the *essence* of what a capitalist economy is. It is because he made exchange-value his basic point of reference that Marx's critical analysis of capitalism was so powerful and penetrating. He saw capitalism as a complex structure of commodity relations, i.e. people relating to one another as buyers and sellers.

Socialists have always been clear enough that what they are looking for is an alternative to capitalism. What has been difficult to find is the alternative practice that points towards *new* economic relations. The essential idea of the capitalist economy is that economic value is measured by exchange-value. Competition gives the prize to methods that produce most exchange value at least cost. This gives a clear measure of 'efficiency' and competitive success or failure provides the hard practical test. The socialist criticism of all this is that economic decisions based on these criteria produce many socially appalling outcomes: mass unemployment, pollution, lack of provision for elementary needs and so forth. But criticism remains just criticism until there is an alternative practice to that prescribed by equating social value to exchange value and the overriding need to sell for money in order to continue as a participant in the economic activity of one's society. *Within* this system as it is, practical economics for workers is primarily about wages and asks few questions about how capabilities are used. Economics, to step away from the 'Wages System' must begin to ask questions about how capabilities are used.

Socialists have somehow thought that 'planning' and 'public ownership' define alternatives. Experience has taught otherwise: these may indeed be necessary conditions for change but they clearly are not sufficient. If one goes back to the day-by-day practice of people, the reasons are not hard to find; these concepts say nothing about the criteria governing decision-making and motivation when people engage in economic activity. The merit of taking commodity relations as the *essence* of capitalism is that they focus light on the criteria and motivations that govern economic activity. Commodity relations are relations between people as buyers and sellers, of which exchange-values, the values they give and receive in exchange, are the expression. Exchange-value measures alternative possibilities and provides criteria for decision-making and the need to possess exchange values, money being their generalised form, motivates economic activity.

The *essential* defect of capitalism is the supremacy accorded to criteria based on exchange-value, that is, money-measures based on values realisable simply through buying and selling. The practical essence of socialist economics turns on the development of economic activities that challenge the supremacy of exchange-value and subordinate the automatisms of the market to criteria of social usefulness. When one thinks a little about it, one soon comes to see that the alternative to the automatisms of the market can only be conscious judgement of social usefulness by human beings. And who best can judge when resources are being well used? It is at this point in the analysis that the economic necessity of democracy becomes apparent: those who produce can best judge the possible ways in which their own activities might be deployed and those whose needs are being met can best judge which products best meet them. In so far as the automatisms of the market are inadequate, people must be able to take control over available resources into their own hands for themselves. The main research assignment for socialist economists should be to explore the practicalities of doing just this in light of the mounting experience of people at the grassroots striving in practice for this goal.

The theoretical concepts that define goals of social change, once discovered, are usually simple and need to be easy to state. Never is it easy, however, to identify day-by-day steps leading towards these ends out of the turmoiled contradictions of the scenes in which we act out our politics. But to begin to find the right moves we need to see our goal and share our vision with others. A socialist vision for the world ahead of us we at present lack. Without this vision appeals for "dedication to full-blooded socialism" are valueless — even counterproductive. When we probe the evangelists of such dedication, we generally find that their 'full-blooded socialism' is nationalisation and planning firmly imposed by a dedicated elite who claim to have seen the light. If, in power, these evangelists prove to be fanatics or crooks, we know only too well the social consequences. Again, when we think about it, the only reliable 'fail-safe mechanism' must be power for the generality of working people to make decisions for themselves. And when social power is analysed, the last line is power to control the use of economic resources: all socialist roads lead back to economic democracy.

What we lack is the locating of this democratic vision of socialism in the centre of the labour movement's political consciousness. Democratic control over resources implies consciousness of possibilities on the part of 'the collective worker' in the workplace organisms and community organisms at the base — where day-by-day our lives as social beings are lived. We need to see consciousness of the social meaning of our collective activities as a socialist duty. And experience has over and over again shewn that such collective awareness immediately awakes visions of better ways to use resources of skill, energy and experience. Such visions educate and trigger action for change. People at the grassroots have been instinctively moving in this direction: of this all the sit-ins and work-ins of the early 1970s were evidence culminating in the work of the Shop Stewards' Combine Committees, 'workers' plans', local employment plans, new forms of co-operatives and community action and much else. What was lacking was complementary work by theoreticians and politicians to bring out the socialist meaning of all these new activities, to make the democratic dimension of socialism central to the labour movement's vision and to swing the movement's organisational assets — the Labour Party in Parliament and local government, the trade unions and trades councils and co-operatives in their 57 varieties — into active furtherance of these grassroot initiatives. The climate is today economically and politically uncongenial, as we all know, but still this remains the central task of the labour movement if real change is to be effected. Again and again logic brings us back to democracy, to staking all on Labour's main asset, that is, people (who *incidentally* are also voters) against capitalism's main asset, that is, control of money in a system that puts exchange-value above what people judge to be of human value.

The need for an adjustment in the labour movement's vision of socialism emerges quite sharply from a critical analysis of the Lucas Aerospace story, by way of example. In 1978 the Labour Party Conference had a lot of resolutions before it about Lucas Aerospace and no voice was raised against the Resolution that it passed in support. But this polite applause masked a total failure to take on board the socialist meaning of the Lucas initiative. The democratic involvement of some 12,000 workers looking at the practicalities of using their resources to better social purposes provided a solid foundation from which to build towards a new form of economic democracy; but obviously as one bit of the economy interacts with others, this could not be done without the support of economic organisations concerned with the British economy as a whole. At that time Labour representatives headed such organisations in government and in the trade unions; but so far from supporting and opening avenues, these necessary apparatuses themselves proved to be obstacles that killed the impetus of the grassroots initiatives. A wonderful opportunity for carrying struggle for economic change into new territories was thrown away. A few years later the defensive capabilities of our apparatuses were no less ineffective and the Lucas management sacked the shop stewards who had been the main architects of these new forms of industrial democracy in practice.

Bureaucracy and careerism and fear of change there certainly is in the labour movement as in all large organisations, but this cannot possibly account for our failures in developing the democratic dimension in socialist economics. This is much more due to our failure to shift the focus of socialist theory and to give out-front political expression to the importance of economic democracy. Economic democracy must become the declared 'accepted wisdom of the labour movement' to complement practical learning and initiatives coming from social organisms at the base. New concepts of socialism appropriate to the times that lie ahead are essential. Politicians and organisers armed with these new concepts will see that the essence of socialist politics is seizing opportunities to enable working people to consciously and collectively appraise their own economic activities, control them and turn them to better social advantage in collaboration with others doing likewise.

Socialism as struggle against the philosophy of exchange-values and commodity-relations does not mean looking for new governments to abolish markets or money or otherwise decree sweeping changes from on high; it means helping people to become aware of the economic processes of which they are part and so to control them. Or, in a word, to subordinate money-values to human values.

Chapter 11

Afterword: Changing the Subject?

Ken Coates

"The Ten Hours Bill...told indeed upon the great contest between the blind role of the supply and demand laws which formed the political economy of the middle class, and social production controlled by social foresight which forms the political economy of the working class. Hence the bill was not only a great political success: it was the victory of a principle: it was the first time in broad daylight the political economy of the middle class succumbed to the political economy of the working class."

Karl Marx

The campaign for industrial democracy is only very partly about elaborating legislative proposals. True, Robert Owen wrote to the Tsar in order to arouse his interest: and none of the reformers who established socialism as a political choice ignored the need for legislative support. But the future of trade unionism depends, in the first place, on its capacity to mobilize opinion, and to encourage people to have confidence in themselves and their own abilities to change the world.

Thus, while one arm of the policy of the trade union movement in Britain must necessarily involve preparing possible legislation for a new Labour Government, the other arm must prepare tomorrow's victories, and win over tomorrow's seasoned campaigners.

Since we live in an international economy which has not yet evolved its proper representative governmental forms, a key part of tomorrow's campaigning involves the creation of grassroots internationalism. Tomorrow's industrial democrats will speak several languages, and work together to administer multinational enterprises. Today's trade unionists, however, need to establish the very beginnings of practical co-operation, on very primary issues.

What could be a more primary issue than that of working time?

Already the European Trade Union Confederation (ETUC) has made this a central issue for collective bargaining in recent years, and has established precise questionnaires and co-ordination in the campaign for a 35-hour week. Some trade union centres have gone beyond this, to call for a maximum week of 32 hours. In Britain, the TUC calls for six weeks annual holiday. Legislation in Austria, Spain, Finland, France, Luxembourg, and Sweden guarantees all workers a minimum of five weeks annual holiday. The scope for systematic campaigning is already large, and has already aroused considerable movements. In considering how these might develop, British trade unions could have received enormous help from one very respected British trade union leader. But, because he died in the middle of 1986, he cannot present these arguments for himself. During the last few months of his life, it was my great good fortune to have several long conversations with Frank Cousins. Even though he was suffering from ill health, his mind was as sharp and keen as ever.

We spent some time talking about the campaign for shorter working hours. I was comparing the courageous but defensive struggle of the miners in Britain with what I saw as, in social terms, the more audacious battle for the shorter working week during the German Metalworkers' dispute. IG Metall, the union which led the strike, had not only advanced conventional industrial relations arguments for shorter working time. It had opened up a broad political campaign aimed at winning general support from women and environmentalist groups as well as trade union members. What was the purpose of shorter hours? Well, how could family relationships be transformed if men were not able to be at home to play their part in child rearing and other domestic work? An increase in 'free' time is quite essential to the improvement of domestic circumstances. It would also have a powerful effect on all kinds of voluntary activities. The German trade unions, in short, took on all the range of arguments about social issues, in order to mobilize general support for their campaign. Of course, shorter working time is very much an issue in the campaign to restore full employment, so the German struggles, closely followed by a dramatic upheaval in Denmark, provided an important example.

Frank Cousins was excited by these developments. "But", he said, "I have been thinking that they need to be given a shape which will lead people forward". "What we need", he said, "is a campaign for the 1000-hour year." I found this idea an electric one. The more I thought about it, the more it had to commend it.

First of all, with unemployment passing 20 million in Western Europe, and bombing along between three and four million in

Britain, we need substantial cuts in working time, as well as economic expansion, if we are not going to be brought to accept the development of an unemployed class of people who are permanently frozen out of the processes of production and community involvement. Of course, Douglas Jay is right when he argues that the extent of human needs on a planetary scale is easily sufficient to generate work for all who want it. But we can't avoid facing another disturbing fact: the very slump which has laid off so many workers has also restricted the application of technologies which would displace even more people, if they were fully applied, flat out. It is therefore no longer a simple humanitarian argument which urges that hours of compulsory labour should be sharply reduced. There is no middle-term solution to the problem of economic regeneration, without an extension of demands by extending employment and free time, taken together.

But in a number of countries, the imposition of agreements about shorter working time runs against barriers in the present day organization of work. Nowhere is this more true than in Britain, where we have established a regime of institutional overtime, as a result of a tacit conspiracy of both management and labour to offset early experiments in incomes policy after the war. Within such a regime of payments, reductions in agreed working hours are very slow to take effect. If one wishes to reduce working time, it would probably be far more effective in such circumstances to increase holiday entitlements, or offer sabbatical leave for various purposes. Of course, longer holidays do not contradict proposals for a shorter working day, or shorter working week. The inestimable merit of the goal of a 1000 hour year is that it leaves wide scope for the development of different approaches, appropriate to the social conditions as well as the organisational needs of different groupings.

The 1000 hours also invite a wide variety of approaches. For any trade union, the 'do-it-yourself' ingredient of policy is crucially important. The political strength of the labour movements depends upon establishing areas in which small-scale reforms are possible, even on a purely experimental basis. Within the wider goal of a 1000 hour year, a 100 different approaches become possible. Groups of workers may bargain for reductions in working time by the day, week or year. Local authorities may agree to extend facilities for their employees, in improving holiday entitlements or the scope for educational leave. National governments may legislate on all these matters, and many others. Legislation can be mandatory, establishing a minimal entitlement or right, or it may be enabling, offering support for the recognition of socially desirable practices. Because there are many roads to the shortening of working time, the overarching goal of the 1000 hours may serve to give people the sense that they are participating in a line of march. It may also serve to knit together workers in widely different trades and industries at widely different levels of skill and technique.

But the 1000 hours can also serve to unite us across frontiers. The stock argument of industrialists against the shorter working week has always been that it would serve to profit the competitive opposition. Convergent action by trade unions in many countries can undermine this resistance. Of course, unions already co-ordinate their schemes, and try to match each other's holiday entitlements, for instance. The 35 hour week, and now the 32 hour week, become standard issues. But the 1000 hour year could become the occasion for a general congress of European labour, involving not only trade union, but also political and community forces. It could deliberately seek to link up with unemployed people, whose aspirations it can help to meet. Trade unions have already established fora in which they can discuss their bargaining strategies: but the 1000 hours implies a co-ordination of political commitment, legislation, and combined social action.

It would be a very fitting memorial to Frank Cousins if we could move towards the first European study conference for a 1000 hour project.

The Contributors

Stephen Bodington
> *Mathematician and economist.*

Ken Coates
> *Reader in Adult Education at Nottingham University, editor Spokesman publications.*

John Edmonds
> *General Secretary, General, Municipal and Boilermakers' Union (GMBATU).*

Bob Fryer
> *Principal of the Northern College, Wentworth.*

Roy Green
> *Research Officer, Labour Party.*

Stuart Holland
> *Shadow Minister for Overseas Development.*

John Hughes
> *Principal of Ruskin College, Oxford.*

Emma MacLennan
> *Research Officer, Labour Party.*

Jim Mortimer
> *Ex-Labour Party General Secretary, former Chairman, Advisory, Conciliation and Arbitration Service (ACAS).*

John Prescott
> *Shadow Minister of Employment.*

Andrew Wilson
> *Senior Lecturer in Law, Polytechnic of the South Bank, London.*

Very Nice Work If You Can Get It

The Socially Useful Production Debate
Edited by Collective Design/Projects

Socially Useful Production seeks to join needs with resources. It spans services, products, labour processes, political demands, political theories and social ideas. No single object, movement or project completely contains and delimits the term. Overall, it relates to the specific needs of particular people: young and old; black and white; men and women; fit and unfit; skilled and unskilled; oppressed and liberated.

Many of the contributors to *Very Nice Work* are centrally involved in recent developments that consciously invoke the aims of Socially Useful Production. They report and celebrate a number of important projects, including initiatives by the Greater London Council, Sheffield City Council and the West Midlands County Council. The editors hope it may provide the basis for a strong, exuberant politics and practice which can both challenge the logics that capital deploys and sustain the growth of oppositional visions and forms.

"This book is stimulating and informative. Its ideas may help us towards a socially useful Government".

Audrey Wise

Contributors:

Cliff Allum	Paul Field	Vin McCabe
Erica Carter	Ursula Huws	Seymour Melman
Cynthia Cockburn	Chris Lee	David Noble
Philip Cooke	Sonia Liff	David Pelly
Mike Cooley	John Lovering	Hilary Wainwright

Illustrated 220pp
Paper £4.95
Cloth £17.50

ISBN 0 85124 431 9
ISBN 0 85124 430 0

SPOKESMAN
Bertrand Russell House, Gamble Street, Nottingham, UK
Tel. 0602 708318

Joint Action for Jobs
A New Internationalism

Edited by Ken Coates, with a foreword by Stuart Weir

Unemployment is laying Europe waste. With twenty million people out of work, the number of direct victims has become intolerable: a common scandal. But there is every reason to believe that this number is growing steadily, whilst the direct sufferers already include whole populations. Yet there is no reason to believe that unemployment is unavoidable or fore-ordained. A mere fraction of the ingenuity which has transformed our technical capacities could re-arrange our social rules in a way which would guarantee a useful role for all our people.

Of course, action by Governments can improve or worsen this condition. If all or even some of the European Governments were willing to act together in order to reject mass unemployment, there is no doubt that conditions could be radically improved. But this is not a problem which can be left to governments. Because it concerns everybody, it needs action by all of us. The work which is necessary requires us to find ways of joining needs to resources, of restructuring institutions to regain the democratic initiative in the global economy. We must find ways to replace the policies of 'beggar my neighbour' by those which seek instead to 'better my neighbour'.

"These excellent essays show how vital it is for socialists who wish to have an impact on unemployment to broaden their horizons, and think internationally".

Ben Pimlott

"Reflecting the thought and experience of those who have already been involved in local enterprise, and building networks to transcend national boundaries, it is an important contribution not only to the debate but to the practical answer to the tens of millions of people without jobs and without the prospect of work in the industrialised world".

David Blunkett

". . . a serious attempt to seek an international solution to some of the major economic problems facing the next Labour Government. It is vital for the Labour Party that it be widely discussed.

Lewis Minkin

Paper £4.95   *ISBN 0 85124 428 9*
Cloth £17.50   *ISBN 0 85124 427 0*
232pp

SPOKESMAN
Bertrand Russell House, Gamble Street, Nottingham, UK
Tel. 0602 708318